The Master Builder

HENRIK IBSEN

DOVER PUBLICATIONS, INC.
Mineola, New York

DOVER THRIFT EDITIONS

GENERAL EDITOR: PAUL NEGRI
EDITOR OF THIS VOLUME: SUSAN L. RATTINER

Copyright

Theatrical Rights

This Dover Thrift Edition may be used in its entirety, in adaptation or in any other way for theatrical productions and performances, professional and amateur, in the United States, without fee, permission, or acknowledgment. (This may not apply outside of the United States, as conditions may vary.)

Bibliographical Note

This Dover edition, first published in 2001 and reissued in 2016, is an unabridged republication of an anonymous translation of the work originally published in 1892. A new introductory Note has been specially prepared for the present edition.

Library of Congress Cataloging-in-Publication Data

Ibsen, Henrik, 1828–1906
   [Bygmester Solness. English]
   The master builder / Henrik Ibsen.
      pages cm (Dover Thrift Editions)
   ISBN-13: 978-0-486-41928-2
   ISBN-10: 0-486-41928-2
   I. Title. II. Series

PT8859 .A312 2001
839.8'226—dc21

2001028960

Manufactured in the United States by RR Donnelley
41928202   2016
www.doverpublications.com

Note

BORN IN A small Norwegian coastal town, Henrik Ibsen (1828–1906) studied medicine as a young man, aspiring one day to become a doctor. He began an apprenticeship as a pharmacy assistant in Grimstad at the age of fifteen, but was unhappy there, and started writing poetry in 1847 as a means of expressing his dispirited feelings. In 1850, he went to Christiania (now Oslo) as a student, where his first verse drama was published under a pen name. Besides editing a weekly newspaper for which he contributed satirical articles, Ibsen launched himself into the dramatist's role with a patriotic verse prologue written specially for the opening of a national theatre in Bergen.

Before his reputation as a playwright soared, Ibsen had accumulated a total of ten years' invaluable experience in all aspects of the theatre, which helped him to develop the necessary tools to write more effectively for the stage. He was stage manager and official poet at the theatre in Bergen for five years—from 1851 until 1856—where he was required to write a minimum of one play a year. From 1857 to 1862, Ibsen spent another five years as director of the Norwegian Theatre in Christiania, but his attempts to improve its standards were frustrated and ended in failure with the close of the theatre. Nevertheless, this decade of practical theatre experience provided Ibsen with the best possible opportunity for perfecting his work, since he learned how to negotiate conflicts with actors, discerned which elements of the production the audience reacted well to, and measured the impact of scenic effects.

In 1864, after writing the poem "A Brother in Need," which urged people to support Denmark in its struggle with Germany, Ibsen left Norway in voluntary exile after his countrymen remained politically apathetic. He wrote the drama *Brand* in Italy, in addition to his famous dramatic masterpiece *Peer Gynt*. During his twenty-seven years abroad, Ibsen also lived in Dresden and Munich before finally returning to Christiania in 1891.

Spanning nearly half a century, the work of Henrik Ibsen startled—

and often offended—the complacent Victorian society of his day. Early critical attention was split squarely down the middle with regard to the groundbreaking nature of his plays, and he was both praised and reviled with equal vehemence for the remainder of his literary career. In spite—and also because—of the controversy he provoked, his work as a dramatist helped promote social reform, as well as altered the conception of dramatic structure as a whole.

Ibsen's psychological dramas mark his shift from a realistic dramatic style (his so-called social plays) to a phase rich in symbolism, best portrayed in his last four plays, *The Master Builder*, *Little Eyolf*, *John Gabriel Borkman*, and *When We Dead Awaken*. Here, his well-honed dramatic style relies primarily on the dichotomy between emotion and intellect that is intrinsic to human nature. His characters, torn by violent conflicts of mind and spirit, are so convincingly real that some critics found his plays to be a shattering look at truth and reality, as they fearlessly exposed the qualities of hypocrisy in both the individual and society.

Contents

Characters

HALVARD SOLNESS, *Master Builder*.
ALINE SOLNESS, *his wife*.
DOCTOR HERDAL, *physician*.
KNUT BROVIK, *formerly an architect, now in* SOLNESS's *employment*.
RAGNAR BROVIK, *his son, draughtsman*.
KAIA FOSLI, *his niece, book-keeper*.
MISS HILDA WANGEL.
Some Ladies.
A Crowd in the street.

The action passes in and about SOLNESS's *house*.

The Master Builder

ACT I

A *plainly furnished work-room in the house of* HALVARD SOLNESS.
*Folding doors on the left lead out to the hall. On the right is the door
leading to the inner rooms of the house. At the back is an open door
into the draughtsmen's office. In front, on the left, a desk with books,
papers and writing materials. Further back than the folding-door, a
stove. In the right-hand corner, a sofa, a table and one or two chairs.
On the table a water-bottle and glass. A smaller table, with a rocking-
chair and arm-chair, in front on the right. Lighted lamps, with
shades, on the table in the draughtsmen's office, on the table in the
corner and on the desk.*

In the draughtsmen's office sit KNUT BROVIK *and his son* RAGNAR, *occu-
pied with plans and calculations. At the desk in the outer office
stands* KAIA FOSLI, *writing in the ledger.* KNUT BROVIK *is a spare old
man with white hair and beard. He wears a rather threadbare but
well-brushed black coat, spectacles and a somewhat discoloured
white neckcloth.* RAGNAR BROVIK *is a well-dressed, light-haired man
in his thirties, with a slight stoop.* KAIA FOSLI *is a slightly built girl,
a little over twenty, carefully dressed and delicate-looking. She has a
green shade over her eyes.——All three go on working for some time
in silence.*

Knut Brovik (*rises suddenly, as if in distress, from the table; breathes
heavily and laboriously as he comes forward into the doorway*).   No, I
can't bear it much longer!

Kaia (*going up to him*).   You are feeling very ill this evening, are
you not, uncle?

Brovik.   Oh, I seem to get worse every day.

Ragnar (*has risen and advances*).   You ought to go home, father. Try
to get a little sleep——

1

Brovik (impatiently).   Go to bed, I suppose? Would you have me sti-
fled outright?

Kaia.   Then take a little walk.

Ragnar.   Yes, do. I will come with you.

Brovik (with warmth).   I will not go till he comes! I am determined
to have it out this evening with—(*in a tone of suppressed bitterness*)—
with him—with the chief.

Kaia (anxiously).   Oh no, uncle—do wait awhile before doing that.

Ragnar.   Yes, better wait, father!

Brovik (draws his breath laboriously).   Ha—ha——! I haven't much
time for waiting.

Kaia (listening).   Hush! I hear him on the stairs.

> [*All three go back to their work. A short silence.* HALVARD SOLNESS
> *comes in through the hall door. He is a man no longer young, but
> healthy and vigorous, with close-cut curly hair, dark moustache
> and dark thick eyebrows. He wears a greyish-green buttoned
> jacket with an upstanding collar and broad lapels. On his head
> he wears a soft grey felt hat, and he has one or two light portfo-
> lios under his arm.*]

*Solness (near the door, points towards the draughtsmen's office, and
asks in a whisper:)*   Are they gone?

Kaia (softly, shaking her head).   No.

> [*She takes the shade off her eyes.* SOLNESS *crosses the room, throws
> his hat on a chair, places the portfolios on the table by the sofa
> and approaches the desk again.* KAIA *goes on writing without in-
> termission, but seems nervous and uneasy.*]

Solness (aloud).   What is that you are entering, Miss Fosli?

Kaia (starts).   Oh, it is only something that——

Solness.   Let me look at it, Miss Fosli. (*Bends over her, pretends to
be looking into the ledger, and whispers:*)   Kaia!

Kaia (softly, still writing).   Well?

Solness.   Why do you always take that shade off when I come?

Kaia (as before).   I look so ugly with it on.

Solness (smiling).   Then you don't like to look ugly, Kaia?

Kaia (half glancing up at him.)   Not for all the world. Not in your
eyes.

Solness (stroking her hair gently).   Poor, poor little Kaia——

Kaia (bending her head).   Hush—they can hear you.

> [SOLNESS *strolls across the room to the right, turns and pauses at
> the door of the draughtsmen's office.*]

Solness. Has any one been here for me?

Ragnar (rising). Yes, the young couple who wants a villa built, out at Lövstrand.

Solness (growling). Oh, those two! They must wait. I am not quite clear about the plans yet.

Ragnar (advancing, with some hesitation). They were very anxious to have the drawings at once.

Solness (as before). Yes, of course—so they all are.

Brovik (looks up). They say they are longing so to get into a house of their own.

Solness. Yes, yes—we know all that! And so they are content to take whatever is offered them. They get a—a roof over their heads—an address—but nothing to call a home. No thank you! In that case, let them apply to somebody else. Tell them that, the next time they call.

Brovik (pushes his glasses up on to his forehead and looks in astonishment at him). To somebody else? Are you prepared to give up the commission?

Solness (impatiently). Yes, yes, yes, devil take it! If that is to be the way of it——. Rather that, than build away at random. *(Vehemently.)* Besides, I know very little about these people as yet.

Brovik. The people are safe enough. Ragnar knows them. He is a friend of the family. Perfectly safe people.

Solness. Oh, safe—safe enough! That is not at all what I mean. Good Lord—don't you understand me either? *(Angrily.)* I won't have anything to do with these strangers. They may apply to whom they please, so far as I am concerned.

Brovik (rising). Do you really mean that?

Solness (sulkily). Yes I do,—For once in a way.

[*He comes forward.* Brovik *exchanges a glance with* Ragnar, *who makes a warning gesture. Then* Brovik *comes into the front room.*]

Brovik. May I have a few words with you?

Solness. Certainly.

Brovik (to Kaia*).* Just go in there for a moment, Kaia.

Kaia (uneasily). Oh, but uncle——

Brovik. Do as I say, child. And shut the door after you.

[Kaia *goes reluctantly into the draughtsmen's office, glances anxiously and imploringly at* Solness, *and shuts the door.*]

Brovik (lowering his voice a little). I don't want the poor children to know how ill I am.

Solness. Yes, you have been looking very poorly of late.

Brovik. It will soon be all over with me. My strength is ebbing—from day to day.

Solness. Won't you sit down?

Brovik. Thanks—may I?

Solness (placing the arm-chair more conveniently). Here—take this chair.—And now?

Brovik (has seated himself with difficulty). Well, you see, it's about Ragnar. That is what weighs most upon me. What is to become of him?

Solness. Of course your son will stay with me as long as ever he likes.

Brovik. But that is just what he does not like. He feels that he cannot stay here any longer.

Solness. Why, I should say he was very well off here. But if he wants more money, I should not mind——

Brovik. No, no! It is not that. *(Impatiently.)* But sooner or later he, too, must have a chance of doing something on his own account.

Solness (without looking at him). Do you think that Ragnar has quite talent enough to stand alone?

Brovik. No, that is just the heartbreaking part of it—I have begun to have my doubts about the boy. For you have never said so much as—as one encouraging word about him. And yet I cannot but think there must be something in him—he can't be without talent.

Solness. Well, but he has learnt nothing—nothing thoroughly, I mean. Except, of course, to draw.

Brovik (looks at him with covert hatred and says hoarsely). You had learned little enough of the business when you were in my employment. But that did not prevent you from setting to work—*(breathing with difficulty)*—and pushing your way up and taking the wind out of my sails—mine, and so many other people's.

Solness. Yes, you see—circumstances favoured me.

Brovik. You are right there. Everything favoured you. But then how can you have the heart to let me go to my grave—without having seen what Ragnar is fit for? And of course I am anxious to see them married, too—before I go.

Solness (sharply). Is it she who wishes it?

Brovik. Not Kaia so much as Ragnar—he talks about it every day. *(Appealingly.)* You must—you must help him to get some independent work now! I must see something that the lad has done. Do you hear?

Solness (peevishly). Hang it, man, you can't expect me to drag commissions down from the moon for him!

Brovik. He has the chance of a capital commission at this very moment. A big bit of work.

Solness (uneasily, startled). Has he?

Brovik. If you would give your consent.

Solness. What sort of work do you mean?

Brovik (with some hesitation). He can have the building of that villa out at Lövstrand.

Solness. That! Why, I am going to build that myself.

Brovik. Oh, you don't much care about doing it.

Solness (flaring up). Don't care! I? Who dares to say that?

Brovik. You said so yourself just now.

Solness. Oh, never mind what I say.—Would they give Ragnar the building of that villa?

Brovik. Yes. You see, he knows the family. And then—just for the fun of the thing—he has made drawings and estimates and so forth——

Solness. Are they pleased with the drawings? The people who will have to live in the house?

Brovik. Yes. If you would only look through them and approve of them.

Solness. Then they would let Ragnar build their home for them?

Brovik. They were immensely pleased with his idea. They thought it exceedingly original, they said.

Solness. Oho! Original! Not the old-fashioned stuff that *I* am in the habit of turning out!

Brovik. It seemed to them different.

Solness (with suppressed irritation). So it was to see Ragnar that they came here—whilst I was out!

Brovik. They came to call upon you—and at the same time to ask whether you would mind retiring——

Solness (angrily). Retire? I?

Brovik. In case you thought that Ragnar's drawings——

Solness. I? Retire in favour of your son!

Brovik. Retire from the agreement, they meant.

Solness. Oh, it comes to the same thing. *(Laughs angrily.)* So that is it, is it? Halvard Solness is to see about retiring now! To make room for younger men! For the very youngest, perhaps! He must make room! Room! Room!

Brovik. Why, good heavens! there is surely room for more than one single man——

Solness. Oh, there's not so very much room to spare either. But, be that as it may—I will never retire! I will never give way to anybody! Never of my own free will. Never in this world will I do that!

Brovik (rises with difficulty). Then I am to pass out of life without any certainty? Without a gleam of happiness? Without any faith or trust in Ragnar? Without having seen a single piece of work of his doing? Is that to be the way of it?

Solness (turns half aside and mutters). H'm—don't ask more just now.

Brovik. I must have an answer to this one question. Am I to pass out of life in such utter poverty?

Solness (seems to struggle with himself; finally he says, in a low but firm voice:) You must pass out of life as best you can.

Brovik. Then be it so.

[*He goes up the room.*]

Solness (following him, half in desperation). Don't you understand that I cannot help it? I am what I am, and I cannot change my nature!

Brovik. No, no; I suppose you can't. *(Reels and supports himself against the sofa-table.)* May I have a glass of water?

Solness. By all means.

[*Fills a glass and hands it to him.*]

Brovik. Thanks.

[*Drinks and puts the glass down again.* SOLNESS *goes up and opens the door of the draughtsmen's office.*]

Solness. Ragnar—you must come and take your father home.

[RAGNAR *rises quickly. He and* KAIA *come into the work-room.*]

Ragnar. What is the matter, father?

Brovik. Give me your arm. Now let us go.

Ragnar. Very well. You had better put your things on, too, Kaia.

Solness. Miss Fosli must stay—just for a moment. There is a letter I want written.

Brovik (looks at SOLNESS*).* Good night. Sleep well—if you can.

Solness. Good night.

[BROVIK *and* RAGNAR *go out by the hall door.* KAIA *goes to the desk.* SOLNESS *stands with bent head, to the right, by the arm-chair.*]

Kaia (dubiously). Is there any letter——?

Solness (curtly). No, of course not. *(Looks sternly at her.)* Kaia!

Kaia (anxiously, in a low voice). Yes!

Solness (points imperatively to a spot on the floor). Come here! At once!

Kaia (hesitatingly). Yes.

Solness (as before). Nearer!

Kaia (obeying). What do you want with me?

Solness (looks at her for a while). Is it you I have to thank for all this?

Kaia.   No, no, don't think that!

Solness.   But confess now—you want to get married!

Kaia (softly).   Ragnar and I have been engaged for four or five years, and so——

Solness.   And so you think it time there were an end to it. Is not that so?

Kaia.   Ragnar and Uncle say I must. So I suppose I shall have to give in.

Solness (more gently).   Kaia, don't you really care a little bit for Ragnar, too?

Kaia.   I cared very much for Ragnar once—before I came here to you.

Solness.   But you don't now? Not in the least?

Kaia (passionately, clasping her hands and holding them out towards him).   Oh, you know very well there is only one person I care for now! One, and one only, in all the world! I shall never care for anyone else.

Solness.   Yes, you say that. And yet you go away from me—leave me alone here with everything on my hands.

Kaia.   But could I not stay with you, even if Ragnar——?

Solness (repudiating the idea).   No, no, that is quite impossible. If Ragnar leaves me and starts work on his own account, then of course he will need you himself.

Kaia (wringing her hands).   Oh, I feel as if I could not be separated from you! It's quite, quite impossible!

Solness.   Then be sure you get those foolish notions out of Ragnar's head. Marry him as much as you please—*(alters his tone.)*—I mean—don't let him throw up his good situation with me. For then I can keep you, too, my dear Kaia.

Kaia.   Oh yes, how lovely that would be, if it could only be managed!

Solness (clasps her head with his two hands and whispers).   For I cannot get on without you, you see. I must have you with me every single day.

Kaia (in nervous exaltation).   My God! My God!

Solness (kisses her hair).   Kaia—Kaia!

Kaia (sinks down before him).   Oh, how good you are to me! How unspeakably good you are!

Solness (vehemently).   Get up! For goodness' sake get up! I think I hear some one!

[*He helps her to rise. She staggers over to the desk. MRS. SOLNESS enters by the door on the right. She looks thin and wasted with grief, but shows traces of bygone beauty. Blonde ringlets. Dressed with good taste, wholly in black. Speaks somewhat slowly and in a plaintive voice.*]

Mrs. Solness (in the doorway).   Halvard!

Solness (turns).   Oh, are you there, my dear——?

Mrs. Solness (with a glance at KAIA).   I am afraid I am disturbing you.

Solness.   Not in the least. Miss Fosli has only a short letter to write.

Mrs. Solness.   Yes, so I see.

Solness.   What do you want with me, Aline?

Mrs. Solness.   I merely wanted to tell you that Dr. Herdal is in the drawing-room. Won't you come and see him, Halvard?

Solness (looks suspiciously at her).   H'm—is the doctor so very anxious to talk to me?

Mrs. Solness.   Well, not exactly anxious. He really came to see me; but he would like to say how-do-you-do to you at the same time.

Solness (laughs to himself).   Yes, I daresay. Well, you must ask him to wait a little.

Mrs. Solness.   Then you will come in presently?

Solness.   Perhaps I will. Presently, presently, dear. In a little while.

Mrs. Solness (glancing again at KAIA).   Well, now, don't forget, Halvard.

[*Withdraws and closes the door behind her.*]

Kaia (softly).   Oh dear, oh dear—I am sure Mrs. Solness thinks ill of me in some way!

Solness.   Oh, not in the least. Not more than usual, at any rate. But all the same, you had better go now, Kaia.

Kaia.   Yes, yes, now I must go.

Solness (severely).   And mind you get that matter settled for me. Do you hear?

Kaia.   Oh, if it only depended on me——

Solness.   I will have it settled, I say! And to-morrow too—not a day later!

Kaia (terrified).   If there's nothing else for it, I am quite willing to break off the engagement.

Solness (angrily).   Break it off? Are you mad? Would you think of breaking it off?

Kaia (distracted).   Yes, if necessary. For I must—I must stay here with you! I can't leave you! That is utterly—utterly impossible!

Solness (with a sudden outburst).   But deuce take it—how about Ragnar then! It's Ragnar that I——

Kaia (looks at him with terrified eyes).   It is chiefly on Ragnar's account, that—that you——

Solness (collecting himself).   No, no, of course not! You don't understand me either. (*Gently and softly.*) Of course it is you I want to keep—you above everything, Kaia. But for that very reason, you must prevent Ragnar, too, from throwing up his situation. There, there,— now go home.

Kaia. Yes, yes—good-night, then.

Solness. Good-night. (*As she is going.*) Oh, stop a moment! Are Ragnar's drawings in there?

Kaia. I did not see him take them with him.

Solness. Then just go and find them for me. I might perhaps glance over them, after all.

Kaia (happy). Oh yes, please do!

Solness. For your sake, Kaia dear. Now, let me have them at once, please.

[KAIA *hurries into the draughtsmen's office, searches anxiously in the table-drawer, finds a portfolio and brings it with her.*]

Kaia. Here are all the drawings.

Solness. Good. Put them down there on the table.

Kaia (putting down the portfolio). Good-night, then. (*Beseechingly.*) And please, please think kindly of me.

Solness. Oh, that I always do. Good-night, my dear little Kaia. (*Glances to the right.*) Go, go now!

[MRS. SOLNESS *and* DR. HERDAL *enter by the door on the right. He is a stoutish, elderly man, with a round, good-humoured face, clean shaven, with thin, light hair, and gold spectacles.*]

Mrs. Solness (still in the doorway). Halvard, I cannot keep the doctor any longer.

Solness. Well then, come in here.

Mrs. Solness (to KAIA, who is turning down the desk-lamp). Have you finished the letter already, Miss Fosli?

Kaia (in confusion). The letter——?

Solness. Yes, it was quite a short one.

Mrs. Solness. It must have been very short.

Solness. You may go now, Miss Fosli. And please come in good time to-morrow morning.

Kaia. I will be sure to. Good-night, Mrs. Solness.

[*She goes out by the hall door.*]

Mrs. Solness. She must be quite an acquisition to you, Halvard, this Miss Fosli.

Solness. Yes, indeed. She is useful in all sorts of ways.

Mrs. Solness. So it seems.

Dr. Herdal. Is she good at book-keeping too?

Solness. Well—of course she has had a good deal of practice during these two years. And then she is so nice and willing to do whatever one asks of her.

Mrs. Solness. Yes, that must be very delightful——

Solness. It is. Especially when one is not too much accustomed to that sort of thing.

Mrs. Solness (in a tone of gentle remonstrance). Can you say that, Halvard?

Solness. Oh, no, no, my dear Aline; I beg your pardon.

Mrs. Solness. There's no occasion.—Well then, doctor, you will come back later on and have a cup of tea with us?

Dr. Herdal. I have only that one patient to see and then I'll come back.

Mrs. Solness. Thank you.

[*She goes out by the door on the right.*]

Solness. Are you in a hurry, doctor?

Dr. Herdal. No, not at all.

Solness. May I have a little chat with you?

Dr. Herdal. With the greatest of pleasure.

Solness. Then let us sit down. (*He motions the doctor to take the rocking-chair and sits down himself in the arm-chair. Looks searchingly at him.*) Tell me—did you notice anything odd about Aline?

Dr. Herdal. Do you mean just now, when she was here?

Solness. Yes, in her manner to me. Did you notice anything?

Dr. Herdal (smiling). Well, I admit—one couldn't well avoid noticing that your wife—h'm——

Solness. Well?

Dr. Herdal. ——that your wife is not particularly fond of this Miss Fosli.

Solness. Is that all? I have noticed that myself.

Dr. Herdal. And I must say I am scarcely surprised at it.

Solness. At what?

Dr. Herdal. That she should not exactly approve of your seeing so much of another woman, all day and every day.

Solness. No, no, I suppose you are right there—and Aline too. But it's impossible to make any change.

Dr. Herdal. Could you not engage a clerk?

Solness. The first man that came to hand? No, thank you—that would never do for me.

Dr. Herdal. But now, if your wife——? Suppose, with her delicate health, all this tries her too much?

Solness. Even then—I might almost say—it can make no difference. I must keep Kaia Fosli. No one else could fill her place.

Dr. Herdal. No one else?

Solness (curtly). No, no one.

Dr. Herdal (drawing his chair closer). Now listen to me, my dear Mr. Solness. May I ask you a question, quite between ourselves?

Solness. By all means.

Dr. Herdal. Women, you see—in certain matters, they have a deucedly keen intuition——

Solness. They have, indeed. There is not the least doubt of that. But——?

Dr. Herdal. Well, tell me now—if your wife can't endure this Kaia Fosli——?

Solness. Well, what then?

Dr. Herdal. ——may she not have just—just the least little bit of reason for this instinctive dislike?

Solness (looks at him and rises). Oho!

Dr. Herdal. Now don't be offended—but hasn't she?

Solness (with curt decision). No.

Dr. Herdal. No reason of any sort?

Solness. No other reason than her own suspicious nature.

Dr. Herdal. I know you have known a good many women in your time.

Solness. Yes, I have.

Dr. Herdal. And have been a good deal taken with some of them, too.

Solness. Oh, yes, I don't deny it.

Dr. Herdal. But as regards Miss Fosli, then? There is nothing of that sort in the case?

Solness. No; nothing at all—on my side.

Dr. Herdal. But on her side?

Solness. I don't think you have any right to ask that question, doctor.

Dr. Herdal. Well, you know, we were discussing your wife's intuition.

Solness. So we were. And for that matter—*(lowers his voice)*—Aline's intuition, as you call it—in a certain sense, it has not been so far astray.

Dr. Herdal. Aha! there we have it!

Solness (sits down). Doctor Herdal—I am going to tell you a strange story—if you care to listen to it.

Dr. Herdal. I like listening to strange stories.

Solness. Very well then. I daresay you recollect that I took Knut Brovik and his son into my employment—after the old man's business had gone to the dogs.

Dr. Herdal. Yes, so I have understood.

Solness. You see, they really are clever fellows, these two. Each of them has talent in his own way. But then the son took it into his head to get engaged; and the next thing, of course, was that he wanted to get married—and begin to build on his own account. That is the way with all these young people.

Dr. Herdal (laughing). Yes, they have a bad habit of wanting to marry.

Solness. Just so. But of course that did not suit my plans; for I needed Ragnar myself—and the old man, too. He is exceedingly good at calculating bearing-strains and cubic contents—and all that sort of devilry, you know.

Dr. Herdal. Oh, yes, no doubt that's indispensable.

Solness. Yes, it is. But Ragnar was absolutely bent on setting to work for himself. He would hear of nothing else.

Dr. Herdal. But he has stayed with you all the same.

Solness. Yes, I'll tell you how that came about. One day this girl, Kaia Fosli, came to see them on some errand or other. She had never been here before. And when I saw how utterly infatuated they were with each other, the thought occurred to me: if I could only get her into the office here, then perhaps Ragnar, too, would stay where he is.

Dr. Herdal. That was not at all a bad idea.

Solness. Yes, but at the time I did not breathe a word of what was in my mind. I merely stood and looked at her—and kept on wishing intently that I could have her here. Then I talked to her a little, in a friendly way—about one thing and another. And then she went away.

Dr. Herdal. Well?

Solness. Well, then, next day, pretty late in the evening, when old Brovik and Ragnar had gone home, she came here again and behaved as if I had made an arrangement with her.

Dr. Herdal. An arrangement? What about?

Solness. About the very thing my mind had been fixed on. But I hadn't said one single word about it.

Dr. Herdal. That was most extraordinary.

Solness. Yes, was it not? And now she wanted to know what she was to do here—whether she could begin the very next morning, and so forth.

Dr. Herdal. Don't you think she did it in order to be with her sweetheart?

Solness. That was what occurred to me at first. But no, that was not it. She seemed to drift quite away from him—when once she had come here to me.

Dr. Herdal. She drifted over to you, then?

Solness. Yes, entirely. If I happen to look at her when her back is turned, I can tell that she feels it. She quivers and trembles the moment I come near her. What do you think of that?

Dr. Herdal. H'm—that's not very hard to explain.

Solness. Well, but what about the other thing? That she believed I had said to her what I had only wished and willed—silently—inwardly—to myself? What do you say to that? Can you explain that, Dr. Herdal?

Dr. Herdal. No, I won't undertake to do that.

Solness. I felt sure you would not; and so I have never cared to talk about it till now. But it's a cursed nuisance to me in the long run, you understand. Here I have to go on day after day pretending——. And it's a shame to treat her so, too, poor girl. *(Vehemently.)* But I cannot do anything else. For if she runs away from me—then Ragnar will be off too.

Dr. Herdal. And you have not told your wife the rights of the story?

Solness. No.

Dr. Herdal. Then why on earth don't you?

Solness (looks fixedly at him, and says in a low voice:) Because I seem to find a sort of—of salutary self-torture in allowing Aline to do me an injustice.

Dr. Herdal (shakes his head). I don't in the least understand what you mean.

Solness. Well, you see—it is like paying off a little bit of a huge, immeasurable debt——

Dr. Herdal. To your wife?

Solness. Yes; and that always helps to relieve one's mind a little. One can breathe more freely for a while, you understand.

Dr. Herdal. No, goodness knows, I don't understand at all——

Solness (breaking off, rises again). Well, well, well—then we won't talk any more about it. *(He saunters across the room, returns and stops beside the table. Looks at the doctor with a sly smile.)* I suppose you think you have drawn me out nicely now, doctor?

Dr. Herdal (with some irritation). Drawn you out? Again I have not the faintest notion what you mean, Mr. Solness.

Solness. Oh come, out with it; I have seen it quite clearly, you know.

Dr. Herdal. What have you seen?

Solness (in a low voice, slowly). That you have been quietly keeping an eye upon me.

Dr. Herdal. That I have! And why in all the world should I do that?

Solness. Because you think that I—— *(Passionately.)* Well, devil take it—you think the same of me as Aline does.

Dr. Herdal. And what does she think about you?

Solness (having recovered his self-control). She has begun to think that I am—that I am—ill.

Dr. Herdal. Ill! You! She has never hinted such a thing to me. Why, what can she think is the matter with you?

Solness (leans over the back of the chair and whispers). Aline has made up her mind that I am mad. That is what she thinks.

Dr. Herdal (rising). Why, my dear good fellow——!

Solness. Yes, on my soul she does! I tell you it is so. And she has got you to think the same! Oh, I can assure you, doctor, I see it in your face as clearly as possible. You don't take me in so easily, I can tell you.

Dr. Herdal (looks at him in amazement). Never, Mr. Solness— never has such a thought entered my mind.

Solness (with an incredulous smile). Really? Has it not?

Dr. Herdal. No, never! Nor your wife's mind either, I am convinced. I could almost swear to that.

Solness. Well, I wouldn't advise you to. For, in a certain sense, you see, perhaps—perhaps she is not so far wrong in thinking something of the kind.

Dr. Herdal. Come now, I really must say——

Solness (interrupting, with a sweep of his hand). Well, well, my dear doctor—don't let us discuss this any further. We had better agree to differ. *(Changes to a tone of quiet amusement.)* But look here now, doctor—h'm——

Dr. Herdal. Well?

Solness. Since you don't believe that I am—ill—and crazy, and mad, and so forth——

Dr. Herdal. What then?

Solness. Then I daresay you fancy that I am an extremely happy man.

Dr. Herdal. Is that mere fancy?

Solness (laughs). No, no—of course not! Heaven forbid! Only think—to be Solness the master builder! Halvard Solness! What could be more delightful?

Dr. Herdal. Yes, I must say it seems to me you have had the luck on your side to an astounding degree.

Solness (suppresses a gloomy smile). So I have, I can't complain on that score.

Dr. Herdal. First of all that grim old robbers' castle was burnt down for you. And that was certainly a great piece of luck.

Solness (seriously). It was the home of Aline's family. Remember that.

Dr. Herdal. Yes, it must have been a great grief to her.

Solness. She has not got over it to this day—not in all these twelve or thirteen years.

Dr. Herdal. Ah, but what followed must have been the worst blow for her.

Solness. The one thing with the other.

Dr. Herdal. But you—yourself—you rose upon the ruins. You began as a poor boy from a country village—and now you are at the head of your profession. Ah, yes, Mr. Solness, you have undoubtedly had the luck on your side.

Solness (looking at him with embarrassment). Yes, but that is just what makes me so horribly afraid.

Dr. Herdal. Afraid? Because you have the luck on your side!

Solness. It terrifies me—terrifies me every hour of the day. For sooner or later the luck must turn, you see.

Dr. Herdal. Oh nonsense! What should make the luck turn?

Solness (with firm assurance). The younger generation.

Dr. Herdal. Pooh! The younger generation! You are not laid on the shelf yet, I should hope. Oh no—your position here is probably firmer now than it has ever been.

Solness. The luck will turn. I know it—I feel the day approaching. Some one or other will take it into his head to say: Give me a chance! And then all the rest will come clamouring after him, and shake their fists at me and shout: Make room—make room—make room! Yes, just you see, doctor—presently the younger generation will come knock at my door——

Dr. Herdal (laughing). Well, and what if they do?

Solness. What if they do? Then there's an end of Halvard Solness.

[*There is a knock at the door on the left.*]

Solness (starts). What's that? Did you not hear something?

Dr. Herdal. Some one is knocking at the door.

Solness (loudly). Come in.

[HILDA WANGEL *enters by the hall door. She is of middle height, supple and delicately built. Somewhat sunburnt. Dressed in a tourist costume, with skirt caught up for walking, a sailor's collar open at the throat and a small sailor hat on her head. Knapsack on back, plaid in strap, and alpenstock.*]

Hilda (goes straight up to SOLNESS, *her eyes sparkling with happiness).* Good evening!

Solness (looks doubtfully at her). Good evening——

Hilda (laughs). I almost believe you don't recognise me!

Solness. No—I must admit that—just for the moment——

Dr. Herdal (approaching). But I recognise you, my dear young lady——

Hilda (pleased). Oh, is it you that——

Dr. Herdal. 'Of course it is. *(To* SOLNESS.*)* We met at one of the mountain stations this summer. *(To* HILDA.*)* What became of the other ladies?

Hilda. Oh, they went westward.

Dr. Herdal. They didn't much like all the fun we used to have in the evenings.

Hilda. No, I believe they didn't.

Dr. Herdal (holds up his finger at her). And I am afraid it can't be denied that you flirted a little with us.

Hilda. Well that was better fun than to sit there knitting stockings with all those old women.

Dr. Herdal (laughs). There I entirely agree with you.

Solness. Have you come to town this evening?

Hilda. Yes, I have just arrived.

Dr. Herdal. Quite alone, Miss Wangel?

Hilda. Oh, yes!

Solness. Wangel? Is your name Wangel?

Hilda (looks in amused surprise at him). Yes, of course it is.

Solness. Then you must be a daughter of the district doctor up at Lysanger?

Hilda (as before). Yes, who else's daughter should I be?

Solness. Oh, then I suppose we met up there, that summer when I was building a tower on the old church.

Hilda (more seriously). Yes, of course it was then we met.

Solness. Well, that is a long time ago.

Hilda (looks hard at him). It is exactly ten years.

Solness. You must have been a mere child then, I should think.

Hilda (carelessly). Well, I was twelve or thirteen.

Dr. Herdal. Is this the first time you have ever been up to town, Miss Wangel?

Hilda. Yes, it is indeed.

Solness. And don't you know any one here?

Hilda. Nobody but you. And of course, your wife.

Solness. So you know her, too?

Hilda. Only a little. We spent a few days together at the sanatorium.

Solness. Ah, up there?

Hilda. She said I might come and pay her a visit if ever I came up to town. *(Smiles.)* Not that that was necessary.

Solness. Odd that she should never have mentioned it.

[HILDA *puts her stick down by the stove, takes off the knapsack and lays it and the plaid on the sofa.* DR. HERDAL *offers to help her.* SOLNESS *stands and gazes at her.*]

Hilda (going towards him).   Well, now I must ask you to let me stay the night here.

Solness.   I am sure there will be no difficulty about that.

Hilda.   For I have no other clothes than those I stand in, except a change of linen in my knapsack. And that has to go to the wash, for it's very dirty.

Solness.   Oh, yes, that can be managed. Now I'll just let my wife know——

Dr. Herdal.   Meanwhile I will go and see my patient.

Solness.   Yes, do; and come again later on.

Dr. Herdal (playfully, with a glance at HILDA).   Oh, that I will, you may be very certain! *(Laughs.)* So your prediction has come true, Mr. Solness!

Solness.   How so?

Dr. Herdal.   The younger generation did come knocking at your door.

Solness (cheerfully).   Yes, but in a very different way from what I meant.

Dr. Herdal.   Very different, yes. That's undeniable.

[*He goes out by the hall door.* SOLNESS *opens the door on the right and speaks into the side room.*]

Solness.   Aline! Will you come in here, please. Here is a friend of yours—Miss Wangel.

Mrs. Solness (appears in the doorway).   Who do you say it is? *(Sees* HILDA.) Oh, is it you, Miss Wangel? *(Goes up to her and offers her hand.)* So you have come to town after all.

Solness.   Miss Wangel has this moment arrived; and she would like to stay the night here.

Mrs. Solness.   Here with us? Oh yes, certainly.

Solness.   Till she can get her things a little in order, you know.

Mrs. Solness.   I will do the best I can for you. It's no more than my duty. I suppose your trunk is coming on later?

Hilda.   I have no trunk.

Mrs. Solness.   Well, it will be all right, I daresay. In the meantime, you must excuse my leaving you here with my husband, until I can get a room made a little comfortable for you.

Solness.   Can we not give her one of the nurseries? They are all ready as it is.

Mrs. Solness. Oh, yes. There we have room and to spare. *(To* HILDA.*)* Sit down now, and rest a little.

[*She goes out to the right.* HILDA, *with her hands behind her back, strolls about the room and looks at various objects.* SOLNESS *stands in front, beside the table, also with his hands behind his back, and follows her with his eyes.*]

Hilda (stops and looks at him). Have you several nurseries?
Solness. There are three nurseries in the house.
Hilda. That's a lot. Then I suppose you have a great many children?
Solness. No. We have no child. But now you can be the child here, for the time being.
Hilda. For to-night, yes. I shall not cry. I mean to sleep as sound as a stone.
Solness. Yes, you must be very tired, I should think.
Hilda. Oh, no! But all the same —— It's so delicious to lie and dream.
Solness. Do you dream much of nights?
Hilda. Oh, yes! Almost always.
Solness. What do you dream about most?
Hilda. I shan't tell you to-night. Another time, perhaps.

[*She again strolls about the room, stops at the desk and turns over the books and papers a little.*]

Solness (approaching). Are you searching for anything?
Hilda. No, I am merely looking at all these things. *(Turns.)* Perhaps I mustn't?
Solness. Oh, by all means.
Hilda. Is it you that write in this great ledger?
Solness. No, it's my book-keeper.
Hilda. Is it a woman?
Solness (smiles). Yes.
Hilda. One you employ here, in your office?
Solness. Yes.
Hilda. Is she married?
Solness. No, she is single.
Hilda. Oh, indeed!
Solness. But I believe she is soon going to be married.
Hilda. That's a good thing for her.
Solness. But not such a good thing for me. For then I shall have nobody to help me.

Hilda. Can't you get hold of some one else who will do just as well?

Solness. Perhaps you would stay here and write in the ledger?

Hilda (measures him with a glance). Yes, I daresay! No, thank you—nothing of that sort for me.

[*She again strolls across the room and sits down in the rocking-chair.* SOLNESS, *too, goes to the table.*]

Hilda (continuing). For there must surely be plenty of other things to be done here. (*Looks smiling at him.*) Don't you think so, too?

Solness. Of course. First of all, I suppose, you want to make a round of the shops and get yourself up in the height of fashion.

Hilda (amused). No, I think I shall let that alone!

Solness. Indeed.

Hilda. For you must know I have run through all my money.

Solness (laughs). Neither trunk nor money, then.

Hilda. Neither one nor the other. But never mind—it doesn't matter now.

Solness. Come now, I like you for that.

Hilda. Only for that?

Solness. For that among other things. (*Sits in the arm-chair.*) Is your father alive still?

Hilda. Yes, father's alive.

Solness. Perhaps you are thinking of studying here?

Hilda. No, that hadn't occurred to me.

Solness. But I suppose you will be staying for some time?

Hilda. That must depend upon circumstances.

[*She sits awhile rocking herself and looking at him, half seriously, half with a suppressed smile. Then she takes off her hat and puts it on the table in front of her.*]

Hilda. Mr. Solness!

Solness. Well?

Hilda. Have you a very bad memory?

Solness. A bad memory? No, not that I am aware of.

Hilda. Then have you nothing to say to me about what happened up there?

Solness (in momentary surprise). Up at Lysanger? (*Indifferently.*) Why, it was nothing much to talk about, it seems to me.

Hilda (looks reproachfully at him). How can you sit there and say such things?

Solness. Well, then, you talk to me about it.

Hilda. When the tower was finished, we had grand doings in the town.

Solness. Yes, I shall not easily forget that day.

Hilda (smiles). Will you not? That comes well from you.

Solness. Comes well?

Hilda. There was music in the churchyard—and many, many hundreds of people. We school-girls were dressed in white; and we all carried flags.

Solness. Ah yes, those flags—I can tell you I remember them!

Hilda. Then you climbed right up the scaffolding, straight to the very top; and you had a great wreath with you; and you hung that wreath right away up on the weather-vane.

Solness (curtly interrupting). I always did that in those days. It was an old custom.

Hilda. It was so wonderfully thrilling to stand below and look up at you. Fancy, if he should fall over! He—the master builder himself!

Solness (as if to divert her from the subject). Yes, yes, yes, that might very well have happened, too. For one of those white-frocked little devils,—she went on in such a way, and screamed up at me so——

Hilda (sparkling with pleasure). "Hurrah for Master Builder Solness!" Yes!

Solness. ——and waved and flourished with her flag, so that I—so that it almost made me giddy to look at it.

Hilda (in a lower voice, seriously). That little devil—that was I.

Solness (fixes his eyes steadily upon her). I am sure of that now. It must have been you.

Hilda (lively again). Oh, it was so gloriously thrilling! I could not have believed there was a builder in the whole world that could build such a tremendously high tower. And then, that you yourself should stand at the very top of it, as large as life! And that you should not be the least bit dizzy! It was that above everything that made one—made one dizzy to think of.

Solness. How could you be so certain that I was not——?

Hilda (scouting the idea). No indeed! Oh, no! I knew that instinctively. For if you had been, you could never have stood up there and sung.

Solness (looks at her in astonishment). Sung? Did *I* sing?

Hilda. Yes, I should think you did.

Solness (shakes his head). I have never sung a note in my life.

Hilda. Yes indeed, you sang then. It sounded like harps in the air.

Solness (thoughtfully). This is very strange—all this.

Hilda (is silent awhile, looks at him and says in a low voice:) But then,—it was after that—and the real thing happened.

Solness. The real thing?

Hilda (sparkling with vivacity). Yes, I surely don't need to remind you of that?

Solness. Oh, yes, do remind me a little of that, too.

Hilda. Don't you remember that a great dinner was given in your honour at the Club?

Solness. Yes, to be sure. It must have been the same afternoon, for I left the place next morning.

Hilda. And from the Club you were invited to come round to our house to supper.

Solness. Quite right, Miss Wangel. It is wonderful how all these trifles have impressed themselves on your mind.

Hilda. Trifles! I like that! Perhaps it was a trifle, too, that I was alone in the room when you came in?

Solness. Were you alone?

Hilda (without answering him). You didn't call me a little devil then?

Solness. No, I suppose I did not.

Hilda. You said I was lovely in my white dress, and that I looked like a little princess.

Solness. I have no doubt you did, Miss Wangel.—And besides—I was feeling so buoyant and free that day——

Hilda. And then you said that when I grew up I should be your princess.

Solness (laughing a little). Dear, dear—did I say that, too?

Hilda. Yes, you did. And when I asked how long I should have to wait, you said that you would come again in ten years—like a troll and carry me off—to Spain or some such place. And you promised you would buy me a kingdom there.

Solness (as before). Yes, after a good dinner one doesn't haggle about the halfpence. But did I really say all that?

Hilda (laughs to herself). Yes. And you told me, too, what the kingdom was to be called.

Solness. Well, what was it?

Hilda. It was to be called the kingdom of Orangia,* you said.

Solness. Well, that was an appetising name.

Hilda. No, I didn't like it a bit; for it seemed as though you wanted to make game of me.

Solness. I am sure that cannot have been my intention.

Hilda. No, I should hope not—considering what you did next——

Solness. What in the world did I do next?

_____

*In the original "Appelsinia," "appelsin" meaning "orange."

Hilda.   Well, that's the finishing touch, if you have forgotten that, too. I should have thought no one could help remembering such a thing as that.

Solness.   Yes, yes, just give me a hint, and then perhaps—— Well——

Hilda (looks fixedly at him).   You came and kissed me, Mr. Solness.

Solness (open-mouthed, rising from his chair).   I did!

Hilda.   Yes, indeed you did. You took me in both your arms, and bent my head back and kissed me—many times.

Solness.   Now really, my dear Miss Wangel——!

Hilda (rises).   You surely cannot mean to deny it?

Solness.   Yes, I do. I deny it altogether!

Hilda (looks scornfully at him).   Oh, indeed!

[*She turns and goes slowly close up to the stove, where she remains standing motionless, her face averted from him, her hands behind her back. Short pause.*]

Solness (goes cautiously up behind her).   Miss Wangel——!

Hilda (is silent and does not move).

Solness.   Don't stand there like a statue. You must have dreamt all this. (*Lays his hand on her arm.*) Now just listen——

Hilda (makes an impatient movement with her arm).

Solness (as a thought flashes upon him).   Or——! Wait a moment! There is something under all this, you may depend!

Hilda (does not move).

Solness (in a low voice, but with emphasis).   I must have thought all that. I must have wished it—have willed it—have longed to do it. And then——. May not that be the explanation?

Hilda (is still silent).

Solness (impatiently).   Oh very well, deuce take it all—then I did it, I suppose.

Hilda (turns her head a little, but without looking at him).   Then you admit it now?

Solness.   Yes—whatever you like.

Hilda.   You came and put your arms around me?

Solness.   Oh, yes!

Hilda.   And bent my head back?

Solness.   Very far back.

Hilda.   And kissed me?

Solness.   Yes, I did.

Hilda.   Many times?

Solness.   As many as ever you like.

Hilda (turns quickly towards him and has once more the sparkling expression of gladness in her eyes).   Well, you see, I got it out of you at last!

Solness *(with a slight smile).*   Yes—just think of my forgetting such a thing as that.

Hilda *(again a little sulky, retreats from him).*   Oh, you have kissed so many people in your time, I suppose.

Solness.   No, you mustn't think that of me. (HILDA *seats herself in the arm-chair.* SOLNESS *stands and leans against the rocking-chair. Looks observantly at her.)* Miss Wangel!

Hilda.   Yes!

Solness.   How was it now? What came of all this—between us two?

Hilda.   Why, nothing more came of it. You know that quite well. For then the other guests came in, and then—bah!

Solness.   Quite so! The others came in. To think of my forgetting that, too!

Hilda.   Oh, you haven't really forgotten anything: you are only a little ashamed of it all. I am sure one doesn't forget things of that kind.

Solness.   No, one would suppose not.

Hilda *(lively again, looks at him).*   Perhaps you have even forgotten what day it was?

Solness.   What day——?

Hilda.   Yes, on what day did you hang the wreath on the tower? Well? Tell me at once!

Solness.   H'm—I confess I have forgotten the particular day. I only knew it was ten years ago. Sometime in the autumn.

Hilda *(nods her head slowly several times).*   It was ten years ago—on the 19th of September.

Solness.   Yes, it must have been about that time. Fancy your remembering that, too! *(Stops.)* But wait a moment——! Yes—it's the 19th of September to-day.

Hilda.   Yes, it is; and the ten years are gone. And you didn't come—as you promised me.

Solness.   Promised you? Threatened, I suppose you mean?

Hilda.   I don't think there was any sort of threat in that.

Solness.   Well then, a little bit of fun.

Hilda.   Was that all you wanted? To make fun of me?

Solness.   Well, or to have a little joke with you. Upon my soul, I don't recollect. But it must have been something of that kind; for you were a mere child then.

Hilda.   Oh, perhaps I wasn't quite such a child either. Not such a mere chit as you imagine.

Solness *(looks searchingly at her).*   Did you really and seriously expect me to come again?

Hilda (conceals a half-teasing smile). Yes, indeed; I did expect that of you.

Solness. That I should come back to your home and take you away with me?

Hilda. Just like a troll—yes.

Solness. And make a princess of you?

Hilda. That's what you promised.

Solness. And give you a kingdom as well?

Hilda (looks up at the ceiling). Why not? Of course it need not have been an actual, every-day sort of kingdom.

Solness. But something else just as good?

Hilda. Yes, at least as good. *(Looks at him a moment.)* I thought, if you could build the highest church-towers in the world, you could surely manage to raise a kingdom of one sort or another as well.

Solness (shakes his head). I can't quite make you out, Miss Wangel.

Hilda. Can you not? To me it seems all so simple.

Solness. No, I can't make up my mind whether you mean all you say, or are simply having a joke with me.

Hilda (smiles). Making fun of you, perhaps? I, too?

Solness. Yes, exactly. Making fun—of both of us. *(Looks at her.)* Is it long since you found out that I was married?

Hilda. I have known it all along. Why do you ask me that?

Solness (lightly). Oh, well, it just occurred to me. *(Looks earnestly at her and says in a low voice.)* What have you come for?

Hilda. I want my kingdom. The time is up.

Solness (laughs involuntarily). What a girl you are!

Hilda (gaily). Out with my kingdom, Mr. Solness! *(Raps with her fingers.)* The kingdom on the table!

Solness (pushing the rocking-chair nearer and sitting down). Now, seriously speaking—what have you come for? What do you really want to do here?

Hilda. Oh, first of all, I want to go around and look at all the things that you have built.

Solness. That will give you plenty of exercise.

Hilda. Yes, I know you have built a tremendous lot.

Solness. I have indeed—especially of late years.

Hilda. Many church-towers among the rest? Immensely high ones?

Solness. No. I build no more church-towers now. Nor churches either.

Hilda. What do you build, then?

Solness. Homes for human beings.

Hilda (reflectively). Couldn't you build a little—a little bit of a church-tower over these homes as well?

Solness (starting). What do you mean by that?

Hilda. I mean—something that points—points up into the free air. With the vane at a dizzy height.

Solness (pondering a little). Strange that you should say that—for that is just what I am most anxious to do.

Hilda (impatiently). Why don't you do it, then?

Solness (shakes his head). No, the people will not have it.

Hilda. Fancy their not wanting it!

Solness (more lightly). But now I am building a new home for myself—just opposite here.

Hilda. For yourself?

Solness. Yes. It is almost finished. And on that there is a tower.

Hilda. A high tower?

Solness. Yes.

Hilda. Very high?

Solness. No doubt people will say it is too high—too high for a dwelling-house.

Hilda. I'll go out and look at that tower the first thing to-morrow morning.

Solness (sits resting his cheek on his hand and gazes at her). Tell me, Miss Wangel—what is your name? Your Christian name, I mean?

Hilda. Why, Hilda, of course.

Solness (as before). Hilda? Indeed?

Hilda. Don't you remember that? You called me Hilda yourself—that day when you misbehaved.

Solness. Did I really?

Hilda. But then you said "little Hilda"; and I didn't like that.

Solness. Oh, you didn't like that, Miss Hilda?

Hilda. No, not at such a time as that. But—"Princess Hilda"—that will sound very well, I think.

Solness. Very well indeed. Princess Hilda of—of—what was to be the name of the kingdom?

Hilda. Pooh! I won't have anything to do with that stupid kingdom. I have set my heart upon quite a different one!

Solness (has leaned back in the chair, still gazing at her). Isn't it strange——? The more I think of it now, the more it seems to me as though I had gone about all these years torturing myself with—h'm——

Hilda. With what?

Solness. With the effort to recover something—some experience, which I seemed to have forgotten. But I never had the least inkling of what it could be.

Hilda. You should have tied a knot in your pocket-handkerchief, Mr. Solness.

Solness. In that case, I should simply have had to go racking my brains to discover what the knot could mean.

Hilda. Oh, yes, I suppose there are trolls of that kind in the world, too.

Solness (rises slowly). What a good thing it is that you have come to me now.

Hilda (looks deeply into his eyes). Is it a good thing?

Solness. For I have been so lonely here. I have been gazing so helplessly at it all. *(In a lower voice.)* I must tell you—I have begun to be so afraid—so terribly afraid of the younger generation.

Hilda (with a little snort of contempt). Pooh—is the younger generation a thing to be afraid of?

Solness. It is indeed. And that is why I have locked and barred myself in. *(Mysteriously.)* I tell you the younger generation will one day come and thunder at my door! They will break in upon me!

Hilda. Then I should say you ought to go out and open the door to the younger generation.

Solness. Open the door?

Hilda. Yes. Let them come in to you on friendly terms, as it were.

Solness. No, no, no! The younger generation—it means retribution, you see. It comes, as if under a new banner, heralding the turn of fortune.

Hilda (rises, looks at him and says with a quivering twitch of her lips). Can I be of any use to you, Mr. Solness?

Solness. Yes, you can indeed! For you, too, come—under a new banner, it seems to me. Youth marshalled against youth——!

[DR. HERDAL *comes in by the hall door.*]

Dr. Herdal. What—you and Miss Wangel here still?

Solness. Yes. We have had no end of things to talk about.

Hilda. Both old and new.

Dr. Herdal. Have you really?

Hilda. Oh, it has been the greatest fun. For Mr. Solness—he has such a miraculous memory. All the least little details he remembers instantly.

[MRS. SOLNESS *enters by the door on the right.*]

Mrs. Solness. Well, Miss Wangel, your room is quite ready for you now.

Hilda. Oh, how kind you are to me!

Solness (to MRS. SOLNESS*).* The nursery?

Mrs. Solness. Yes, the middle one. But first let us go in to supper.

Solness (nods to HILDA*).* Hilda shall sleep in the nursery, she shall.

Mrs. Solness (looks at him). Hilda?

Solness. Yes, Miss Wangel's name is Hilda. I knew her when she was a child.

Mrs. Solness. Did you really, Halvard? Well, shall we go? Supper is on the table.

[*She takes* DR. HERDAL's *arm and goes out with him to the right.* HILDA *has meanwhile been collecting her travelling things.*]

Hilda (softly and rapidly to SOLNESS*).* Is it true, what you said? Can I be of use to you?

Solness (takes the things from her). You are the very being I have needed most.

Hilda (looks at him with happy, wondering eyes and clasps her hands). But then, great heavens——!

Solness (eagerly). What——?

Hilda. Then I have my kingdom!

Solness (involuntarily). Hilda——!

Hilda (again with the quivering twitch of her lips). Almost—I was going to say.

[*She goes out to the right,* SOLNESS *follows her.*]

ACT II

A prettily furnished small drawing-room in SOLNESS's house. In the back,
a glass door leading out to the verandah and garden. The right-hand
corner is cut off transversely by a large bay-window, in which are
flower-stands. The left-hand corner is similarly cut off by a transverse
wall, in which is a small door papered like the wall. On each side,
an ordinary door. In front, on the right, a console table with a large
mirror over it. Well-filled stands of plants and flowers. In front, on
the left, a sofa with a table and chairs. Further back, a bookcase.
Well forward in the room, before the bay-window, a small table and
some chairs. It is early in the day.

SOLNESS sits by the little table with RAGNAR BROVIK's portfolio open in
front of him. He is turning the drawings over and closely examining
some of them. MRS. SOLNESS moves about noiselessly with a small
watering-pot, attending to her flowers. She is dressed in black as before. Her hat, cloak and parasol lie on a chair near the mirror.
Unobserved by her, SOLNESS now and again follows her with his
eyes. Neither of them speaks.

KAIA FOSLI enters quietly by the door on the left.

Solness (turns his head, and says in an off-hand tone of indifference).
Well, is that you?

Kaia.   I merely wished to let you know that I have come.

Solness.   Yes, yes, that's all right. Hasn't Ragnar come, too?

Kaia.   No, not yet. He had to wait a little while to see the doctor.
But he is coming presently to hear ——

Solness.   How is the old man to-day?

Kaia.   Not well. He begs you to excuse him; he is obliged to keep
his bed to-day.

28

Solness.   Why, of course; by all means let him rest. But now, get to work.

Kaia.   Yes. *(Pauses at the door.)* Do you wish to speak to Ragnar when he comes?

Solness.   No—I don't know that I have anything particular to say to him.

[KAIA *goes out again to the left.* SOLNESS *remains seated, turning over the drawings.*]

Mrs. Solness (over beside the plants).   I wonder if he isn't going to die now, as well?

Solness (looks up to her).   As well as who?

Mrs. Solness (without answering).   Yes, yes—depend upon it, Halvard, old Brovik is going to die, too. You'll see that he will.

Solness.   My dear Aline, ought you not to go out for a little walk?

Mrs. Solness.   Yes, I suppose I ought to.

[*She continues to attend to the flowers.*]

Solness (bending over the drawings).   Is she still asleep?

Mrs. Solness (looking at him).   Is it Miss Wangel you are sitting there thinking about?

Solness (indifferently).   I just happened to recollect her.

Mrs. Solness.   Miss Wangel was up long ago.

Solness.   Oh, was she?

Mrs. Solness.   When I went in to see her, she was busy putting her things in order.

[*She goes in front of the mirror and slowly begins to put on her hat.*]

Solness (after a short pause).   So we have found a use for one of our nurseries after all, Aline.

Mrs. Solness.   Yes, we have.

Solness.   That seems to me better than to have them all standing empty.

Mrs. Solness.   That emptiness is dreadful; you are right there.

Solness (closes the portfolio, rises and approaches her).   You will find that we shall get on far better after this, Aline. Things will be more comfortable. Life will be easier—especially for you.

Mrs. Solness (looks at him).   After this?

Solness.   Yes, believe me, Aline——

Mrs. Solness.   Do you mean—because she has come here?

Solness (checking himself).   I mean, of course—when once we have moved into the new house.

Mrs. Solness (takes her cloak).   Ah, do you think so, Halvard? Will it be better then?

Solness.   I can't think otherwise. And surely you think so, too?

Mrs. Solness.   I think nothing at all about the new house.

Solness (cast down).   It's hard for me to hear you say that; for you know it is mainly for your sake that I have built it.

[*He offers to help her on with her cloak.*]

Mrs. Solness (evades him).   The fact is, you do far too much for my sake.

Solness (with a certain vehemence).   No, no, you really mustn't say that, Aline! I cannot bear to hear you say such things!

Mrs. Solness.   Very well, then I won't say it, Halvard.

Solness.   But I stick to what *I* said. You'll see that things will be easier for you in the new place.

Mrs. Solness.   O heavens—easier for me——!

Solness (eagerly).   Yes, indeed they will! You may be quite sure of that! For you see—there will be so very, very much there that will remind you of your own home——

Mrs. Solness.   The home that used to be father's and mother's—and that was burnt to the ground——

Solness (in a low voice).   Yes, yes, my poor Aline. That was a terrible blow for you.

Mrs. Solness (breaking out in lamentation).   You may build as much as ever you like, Halvard—you can never build up again a real home for me!

Solness (crosses the room).   Well, in heaven's name, let us talk no more about it, then.

Mrs. Solness.   Oh, yes, Halvard, I understand you very well. You are so anxious to spare me—and to find excuses for me, too—as much as ever you can.

Solness (with astonishment in his eyes).   You! Is it you—yourself, that you are talking about, Aline?

Mrs. Solness.   Yes, who else should it be but myself?

Solness (involuntarily to himself).   That, too!

Mrs. Solness.   As for the old house, I wouldn't mind so much about that. When once misfortune was in the air—why——

Solness.   Ah, you are right there. Misfortune will have its way—as the saying goes.

Mrs. Solness.   But it's what came of the fire—the dreadful thing that followed——! That is the thing! That, that, that!

Solness (vehemently).   Don't think about that, Aline!

Mrs. Solness.   Ah, that is exactly what I cannot help thinking about. And now, at last, I must speak about it, too; for I don't seem able to bear it any longer. And then never to be able to forgive myself——

Solness (exclaiming). Yourself——!

Mrs. Solness. Yes, for I had duties on both sides—both towards you and towards the little ones. I ought to have hardened myself—not to have let the horror take such hold upon me—nor the grief for the burning of my old home. *(Wrings her hands.)* Oh, Halvard, if I had only had the strength!

Solness (softly, much moved, comes closer). Aline—you must promise me never to think these thoughts any more.—Promise me that, dear!

Mrs. Solness. Oh, promise, promise! One can promise anything.

Solness (clenches his hands and crosses the room). Oh, but this is hopeless, hopeless! Never a ray of sunlight! Not so much as a gleam of brightness to light up our home!

Mrs. Solness. This is no home, Halvard.

Solness. Oh no, you may well say that. *(Gloomily.)* And God knows whether you are not right in saying that it will be no better for us in the new house, either.

Mrs. Solness. It will never be any better. Just as empty—just as desolate—there as here.

Solness (vehemently). Why in all the world have we built it then? Can you tell me that?

Mrs. Solness. No; you must answer the question for yourself.

Solness (glances suspiciously at her). What do you mean by that, Aline?

Mrs. Solness. What do I mean?

Solness. Yes, in the devil's name! You said it so strangely—as if you had hidden some meaning in it.

Mrs. Solness. No, indeed, I assure you——

Solness (comes closer). Oh, come now—I know what I know. I have both my eyes and my ears about me, Aline—you may depend upon that!

Mrs. Solness. Why, what are you talking about? What is it?

Solness (places himself in front of her). Do you mean to say you don't find a kind of lurking, hidden meaning in the most innocent word I happen to say?

Mrs. Solness. I, do you say? I do that?

Solness (laughs). Ho-ho-ho! It's natural enough, Aline! When you have a sick man on your hands——

Mrs. Solness (anxiously). Sick? Are you ill, Halvard?

Solness (violently). A half-mad man then! A crazy man! Call me what you will.

Mrs. Solness (feels blindly for a chair and sits down). Halvard—for God's sake——

Solness. But you are wrong, both you and the doctor. I am not in the state you imagine.

[*He walks up and down the room.* MRS. SOLNESS *follows him anxiously with her eyes. Finally he goes up to her.*]

Solness (calmly). In reality there is nothing whatever the matter with me.

Mrs. Solness. No, there isn't, is there? But then what is it that troubles you so?

Solness. Why this, that I often feel ready to sink under this terrible burden of debt——

Mrs. Solness. Debt, do you say? But you owe no one anything, Halvard!

Solness (softly, with emotion). I owe a boundless debt to you—to you—to you, Aline.

Mrs. Solness (rises slowly). What is behind all this? You may just as well tell me at once.

Solness. But there is nothing behind it; I have never done you any wrong—not wittingly and wilfully, at any rate. And yet—and yet it seems as though a crushing debt rested upon me and weighed me down.

Mrs. Solness. A debt to me?

Solness. Chiefly to you.

Mrs. Solness. Then you are—ill after all, Halvard.

Solness (gloomily). I suppose I must be—or not far from it. *(Looks towards the door to the right, which is opened at this moment.)* Ah! now it grows lighter.

[HILDA WANGEL *comes in. She has made some alteration in her dress and let down her skirt.*]

Hilda. Good morning, Mr. Solness!

Solness (nods). Slept well?

Hilda. Quite deliciously! Like a child in a cradle. Oh—I lay and stretched myself like—like a princess!

Solness (smiles a little). You were thoroughly comfortable then?

Hilda. I should think so.

Solness. And no doubt you dreamed, too.

Hilda. Yes, I did. But that was horrid.

Solness. Was it?

Hilda. Yes, for I dreamed I was falling over a frightfully high, sheer precipice. Do you never have that kind of dream?

Solness. Oh yes—now and then——

Hilda. It's tremendously thrilling—when you fall and fall——

Solness.   It seems to make one's blood run cold.

Hilda.   Do you draw your legs up under you while you are falling?

Solness.   Yes, as high as ever I can.

Hilda.   So do I.

Mrs. Solness (takes her parasol).   I must go into town now, Halvard. *(To* HILDA.*)* And I'll try to get one or two things that you may require.

Hilda (making a motion to throw her arms round her neck).   Oh, you dear, sweet Mrs. Solness! You are really much too kind to me! Frightfully kind——

Mrs. Solness (deprecatingly, freeing herself).   Oh, not at all. It's only my duty, so I am very glad to do it.

Hilda (offended, pouts).   But really, I think I am quite fit to be seen in the streets—now that I've put my dress to rights. Or do you think I am not?

Mrs. Solness.   To tell you the truth, I think people would stare at you a little.

Hilda (contemptuously).   Pooh! Is that all? That only amuses me.

Solness (with suppressed ill-humour).   Yes, but people might take it into their heads that you were mad, too, you see.

Hilda.   Mad? Are there so many mad people here in town, then?

Solness (points to his own forehead).   Here you see one, at all events.

Hilda.   You—Mr. Solness!

Mrs. Solness.   Oh, don't talk like that, my dear Halvard!

Solness.   Have you not noticed that yet?

Hilda.   No, I certainly have not. *(Reflects and laughs a little.)* And yet—perhaps in one single thing.

Solness.   Ah, do you hear that, Aline?

Mrs. Solness.   What is that one single thing, Miss Wangel?

Hilda.   No, I won't say.

Solness.   Oh, yes, do!

Hilda.   No, thank you—I am not so mad as that.

Mrs. Solness.   When you and Miss Wangel are alone, I daresay she will tell you, Halvard.

Solness.   Ah—you think she will?

Mrs. Solness.   Oh, yes, certainly. For you have known her so well in the past. Ever since she was a child—you tell me.

[*She goes out by the door on the left.*]

Hilda (after a little while).   Does your wife dislike me very much?

Solness.   Did you think you noticed anything of the kind?

Hilda.   Did you not notice it yourself?

Solness (evasively).   Aline has become exceedingly shy with strangers of late years.

Hilda.   Has she really?

Solness.   But if only you could get to know her thoroughly——! Ah! she is so good—so kind—so excellent a creature——

Hilda (impatiently).   But if she is all that—what made her say that about her duty?

Solness.   Her duty?

Hilda.   She said that she would go out and buy something for me, because it was her duty. Oh, I can't bear that ugly, horrid word!

Solness.   Why not?

Hilda.   It sounds so cold and sharp and stinging. Duty—duty—duty. Don't you think so, too? Doesn't it seem to sting you?

Solness.   H'm—haven't thought much about it.

Hilda.   Yes, it does. And if she is so good—as you say she is—why should she talk in that way?

Solness.   But, good Lord, what would you have had her say, then?

Hilda.   She might have said she would do it because she had taken a tremendous fancy to me. She might have said something like that— something really warm and cordial, you understand.

Solness (looks at her).   Is that how you would like to have it?

Hilda.   Yes, precisely. (*She wanders about the room, stops at the bookcase and looks at the books.*) What a lot of books you have.

Solness.   Yes, I have got together a good many.

Hilda.   Do you read them all, too?

Solness.   I used to try to. Do you read much?

Hilda.   No, never! I have given it up. For it all seems so irrelevant.

Solness.   That is just my feeling.

   [HILDA *wanders about a little, stops at the small table, opens the portfolio and turns over the contents.*]

Hilda.   Are all these drawings yours?

Solness.   No, they are drawn by a young man whom I employ to help me.

Hilda.   Some one you have taught?

Solness.   Oh, yes, no doubt he has learnt something from one, too.

Hilda (sits down).   Then I suppose he is very clever. (*Looks at a drawing.*) Isn't he?

Solness.   Oh, he might be worse. For my purpose——

Hilda.   Oh, yes—I'm sure he is frightfully clever.

Solness.   Do you think you can see that in the drawings?

Hilda.   Pooh—these scrawlings! But if he has been learning from you——

Solness.   Oh, so far as that goes—there are plenty of people that have learnt from me and have come to little enough for all that.

Hilda (looks at him and shakes her head). No, I can't for the life of me understand how you can be so stupid.

Solness. Stupid? Do you think I am so very stupid?

Hilda. Yes, I do indeed. If you are content to go about here teaching all these people——

Solness (with a slight start). Well, and why not?

Hilda (rises, half serious, half laughing). No indeed, Mr. Solness! What can be the good of that? No one but you should be allowed to build. You should stand quite alone—do it all yourself. Now you know it.

Solness (involuntarily). Hilda——!

Hilda. Well!

Solness. How in the world did that come into your head?

Hilda. Do you think I am so very far wrong, then?

Solness. No, that's not what I mean. But now I'll tell you something.

Hilda. Well?

Solness. I keep on—incessantly—in silence and alone—brooding on that very thought.

Hilda. Yes, that seems to me perfectly natural.

Solness (looks somewhat searchingly at her). Perhaps you have noticed it already?

Hilda. No, indeed I haven't.

Solness. But just now—when you said you thought I was—off my balance? In one thing, you said——

Hilda. Oh, I was thinking of something quite different.

Solness. What was it?

Hilda. I am not going to tell you.

Solness (crosses the room). Well, well—as you please. (Stops at the bow-window.) Come here, and I will show you something.

Hilda (approaching). What is it?

Solness. Do you see—over there in the garden——?

Hilda. Yes?

Solness (points). Right above the great quarry——?

Hilda. That new house, you mean?

Solness. The one that is being built, yes. Almost finished.

Hilda. It seems to have a very high tower.

Solness. The scaffolding is still up.

Hilda. Is that your new house?

Solness. Yes.

Hilda. The house you are soon going to move into?

Solness. Yes.

Hilda (looks at him). Are there nurseries in that house, too?

Solness.   Three, as there are here.

Hilda.   And no child.

Solness.   And there never will be one.

Hilda (with a half-smile).   Well, isn't it just as I said——?

Solness.   That——?

Hilda.   That you are a little—a little mad after all.

Solness.   Was that what you were thinking of?

Hilda.   Yes, of all the empty nurseries I slept in.

Solness (lowers his voice).   We have had children—Aline and I.

Hilda (looks eagerly at him).   Have you——?

Solness.   Two little boys. They were of the same age.

Hilda.   Twins, then.

Solness.   Yes, twins. It's eleven or twelve years ago now.

Hilda (cautiously).   And so both of them——? You have lost both the twins, then?

Solness (with quiet emotion).   We kept them only about three weeks. Or scarcely so much. *(Bursts forth.)* Oh, Hilda, I can't tell you what a good thing it is for me that you have come! For now at last I have some one I can talk to!

Hilda.   Can you not talk to—her, too?

Solness.   Not about this. Not as I want to talk and must talk. *(Gloomily.)* And not about so many other things, either.

Hilda (in a subdued voice).   Was that all you meant when you said you needed me?

Solness.   That was mainly what I meant—at all events, yesterday. For to-day I am not so sure—— *(Breaking off.)* Come here and let us sit down, Hilda. Sit there on the sofa—so that you can look into the garden. (HILDA *seats herself in the corner of the sofa.* SOLNESS *brings a chair closer.)* Should you like to hear about it?

Hilda.   Yes, I shall love to sit and listen to you.

Solness (sits down).   Then I will tell you all about it.

Hilda.   Now I can see both the garden and you, Mr. Solness. So now, tell away! Begin!

Solness (points towards the bow-window).   Out there on the rising ground—where you see the new house——

Hilda.   Yes?

Solness.   Aline and I lived there in the first years of our married life. There was an old house up there that had belonged to her mother; and we inherited it, and the whole of the great garden with it.

Hilda.   Was there a tower on that house, too?

Solness.   No, nothing of the kind. From the outside it looked like a great, dark, ugly wooden box; but all the same, it was snug and comfortable enough inside.

Hilda. Then did you pull down the ramshackle old place?

Solness. No, it burnt down.

Hilda. The whole of it?

Solness. Yes.

Hilda. Was that a great misfortune for you?

Solness. That depends on how you look at it. As a builder, the fire was the making of me——

Hilda. Well, but——?

Solness. It was just after the birth of the two little boys——

Hilda. The poor little twins, yes.

Solness. They came healthy and bonny into the world. And they were growing too—you could see the difference from day to day.

Hilda. Little children do grow quickly at first.

Solness. It was the prettiest sight in the world to see Aline lying with the two of them in her arms.—But then came the night of the fire——

Hilda (excitedly). What happened? Do tell me! Was any one burnt?

Solness. No, not that. Every one got safe and sound out of the house——

Hilda. Well, and what then——?

Solness. The fright had shaken Aline terribly. The alarm—the escape—the break-neck hurry—and then the ice-cold night air—for they had to be carried out just as they lay—both she and the little ones.

Hilda. Was it too much for them?

Solness. Oh no, they stood it well enough. But Aline fell into a fever, and it affected her milk. She would insist on nursing them herself; because it was her duty, she said. And both our little boys, they— *(clenching his hands.)*—they—oh!

Hilda. They did not get over that?

Solness. No, that they did not get over. That was how we lost them.

Hilda. It must have been terribly hard for you.

Solness. Hard enough for me; but ten times harder for Aline. *(Clenching his hands in suppressed fury.)* Oh, that such things should be allowed to happen here in the world! *(Shortly and firmly.)* From the day I lost them, I had no heart for building churches.

Hilda. Did you not like the church-tower in our town?

Solness. I didn't like it. I know how free and happy I felt when the tower was finished.

Hilda. I know that, too.

Solness. And now I shall never—never build anything of that sort again. Neither churches nor church-towers.

Hilda (nods slowly). Nothing but houses for people to live in.

Solness.   Homes for human beings, Hilda.

Hilda.   But homes with high towers and pinnacles upon them.

Solness.   If possible. (*Adopts a lighter tone.*) But, as I said before, that fire was the making of me—as a builder, I mean.

Hilda.   Why don't you call yourself an architect, like the others?

Solness.   I have not been systematically enough taught for that. Most of what I know, I have found out for myself.

Hilda.   But you succeeded all the same.

Solness.   Yes, thanks to the fire. I laid out almost the whole of the garden in villa lots; and there I was able to build after my own heart. So I came to the front with a rush.

Hilda (looks keenly at him).   You must surely be a very happy man, as matters stand with you.

Solness (gloomily).   Happy? Do you say that, too—like all the rest of them?

Hilda.   Yes, I should say you must be. If you could only cease thinking about the two little children——

Solness (slowly).   The two little children—they are not so easy to forget, Hilda.

Hilda (somewhat uncertainly).   Do you still feel their loss so much—after all these years?

Solness (looks fixedly at her, without replying).   A happy man you said——

Hilda.   Well, now, are you not happy—in other respects?

Solness (continues to look at her).   When I told you all this about the fire—h'm——

Hilda.   Well?

Solness.   Was there not one special thought that you—that you seized upon?

Hilda (reflects in vain).   No. What thought should that be?

Solness (with subdued emphasis).   It was simply and solely by that fire that I was enabled to build homes for human beings. Cosy, comfortable, bright homes, where father and mother and the whole troop of children can live in safety and gladness, feeling what a happy thing it is to be alive in the world—and most of all to belong to each other—in great things and in small.

Hilda (ardently).   Well, and is it not a great happiness for you to be able to build such beautiful homes?

Solness.   The price, Hilda! The terrible price I had to pay for the opportunity!

Hilda.   But can you never get over that?

Solness.   No. That I might build homes for others, I had to forego—to forego for all time—the home that might have been my own. I mean a home for a troop of children—and for father and mother, too.

Hilda (cautiously). But need you have done that? For all time, you say?

Solness (nods slowly). That was the price of this happiness that people talk about. *(Breathes heavily.)* This happiness—h'm—this happiness was not to be bought any cheaper, Hilda.

Hilda (as before). But may it not come right even yet?

Solness. Never in this world—never. That is another consequence of the fire—and of Aline's illness afterwards.

Hilda (looks at him with an indefinable expression). And yet you build all these nurseries?

Solness (seriously). Have you never noticed, Hilda, how the impossible—how it seems to beckon and cry aloud to one?

Hilda (reflecting). The impossible? *(With animation.)* Yes, indeed! Is that how you feel too?

Solness. Yes, I do.

Hilda. There must be—a little of the troll in you, too.

Solness. Why of the troll?

Hilda. What would you call it, then?

Solness (rises). Well, well, perhaps you are right. *(Vehemently.)* But how can I help turning into a troll, when this is how it always goes with me in everything—in everything!

Hilda. How do you mean?

Solness (speaking low, with inward emotion). Mark what I say to you, Hilda. All that I have succeeded in doing, building, creating—all the beauty, security, cheerful comfort—ay, and magnificence, too— *(Clenches his hands.)* Oh, is it not terrible even to think of——!

Hilda. What is so terrible?

Solness. That all this I have to make up for, to pay for—not in money, but in human happiness. And not with my own happiness only, but with other people's, too. Yes, yes, do you see that, Hilda? That is the price which my position as an artist has cost me—and others. And every single day I have to look on while the price is paid for me anew. Over again, and over again—and over again for ever!

Hilda (rises and looks steadily at him). Now I can see that you are thinking of—of her.

Solness. Yes, mainly of Aline. For Aline—she, too, had her vocation in life, just as much as I had mine. *(His voice quivers.)* But her vocation has had to be stunted, and crushed and shattered—in order that mine might force its way to—to a sort of great victory. For you must know that Aline—she, too, had a talent for building.

Hilda. She! For building?

Solness (shakes her head).   Not houses and towers, and spires—not such things as I work away at——

Hilda.   Well, but what then?

Solness (softly, with emotion).   For building up the souls of little children, Hilda. For building up children's souls in perfect balance, and in noble and beautiful forms. For enabling them to soar up into erect and full-grown human souls. That was Aline's talent. And there it all lies now—— unused and unusable for ever—of no earthly service to any one—just like the ruins left by a fire.

Hilda.   Yes, but even if this were so——?

Solness.   It is so! It is so! I know it!

Hilda.   Well, but in any case it is not your fault.

Solness (fixes his eyes on her and nods slowly).   Ah, that is the great, terrible question. That is the doubt that is gnawing me—night and day.

Hilda.   That?

Solness.   Yes. Support the fault was mine—in a certain sense.

Hilda.   Your fault! The fire!

Solness.   All of it; the whole thing. And yet, perhaps—I may not have had anything to do with it.

Hilda (looks at him with a troubled expression).   Oh, Mr. Solness— if you can talk like that, I am afraid you must be—ill, after all.

Solness.   H'm—I don't think I shall ever be of quite sound mind on that point.

[RAGNAR BROVIK *cautiously opens the little door in the left-hand corner.* HILDA *comes forward.*]

Ragnar (when he sees HILDA).   Oh. I beg pardon, Mr. Solness— [*He makes a movement to withdraw.*]

Solness.   No, no, don't go. Let us get it over.

Ragnar.   Oh, yes—if only we could.

Solness.   I hear your father is no better?

Ragnar.   Father is fast growing weaker—and therefore I beg and implore you to write a few kind words for me on one of the plans! Something for father to read before he——

Solness (vehemently).   I won't hear anything more about those drawings of yours!

Ragnar.   Have you looked at them?

Solness.   Yes—I have.

Ragnar.   And they are good for nothing? And *I* am good for nothing, too?

Solness (evasively).   Stay here with me, Ragnar. You shall have everything your own way. And then you can marry Kaia and live at your ease—and happily, too, who knows? Only don't think of building on your own account.

Ragnar.   Well, well, then I must go home and tell father what you say—I promised I would.—Is this what I am to tell father—before he dies?

Solness (with a groan).   Oh tell him—tell him what you will, for me. Best to say nothing at all to him! *(With a sudden outburst).* I cannot do anything else, Ragnar!

Ragnar.   May I have the drawings to take with me?

Solness.   Yes, take them—take them by all means! They are lying there on the table.

Ragnar (goes to the table).   Thanks.

Hilda (puts her hand on the portfolio).   No, no; leave them here.

Solness.   Why?

Hilda.   Because I want to look at them, too.

Solness.   But you have been—— *(To* RAGNAR*).* Well, leave them here, then.

Ragnar.   Very well.

Solness.   And go home at once to your father.

Ragnar.   Yes. I suppose I must.

Solness (as if in desperation).   Ragnar—you must not ask me to do what is beyond my power! Do you hear, Ragnar? You must not!

Ragnar.   No, no. I beg your pardon——

> [*He bows and goes out by the corner door.* HILDA *goes over and sits down on a chair near the mirror.*]

Hilda (looks angrily at SOLNESS*).*   That was a very ugly thing to do.

Solness.   Do you think so, too?

Hilda.   Yes, it was horrible ugly—and hard and bad and cruel as well.

Solness.   Oh, you don't understand my position.

Hilda.   No matter——. I say you ought not to be like that.

Solness.   You said yourself, only just now, that no one but *I* ought to be allowed to build.

Hilda.   *I* may say such things—but you must not.

Solness.   I most of all, surely, who have paid so dear for my position.

Hilda.   Oh yes—with what you call domestic comfort—and that sort of thing.

Solness.   And with my peace of soul into the bargain.

Hilda (rising).   Peace of soul! *(With feeling.)* Yes, yes, you are right in that! Poor Mr. Solness—you fancy that——

Solness (with a quiet, chuckling laugh).   Just sit down again, Hilda, and I'll tell you something funny.

Hilda (sits down; with intent interest).   Well?

Solness.   It sounds such a ludicrous little thing; for, you see, the whole story turns upon nothing but a crack in a chimney.

Hilda.   No more than that?

Solness.   No, not to begin with.

[*He moves a chair nearer to* HILDA *and sits down.*]

Hilda (impatiently, taps on her knee).   Well, now for the crack in the chimney!

Solness.   I had noticed the split in the flue long, long before the fire. Every time I went up into the attic, I looked to see if it was still there.

Hilda.   And it was?

Solness.   Yes; for no one else knew about it.

Hilda.   And you said nothing?

Solness.   Nothing.

Hilda.   And did not think of repairing the flue either?

Solness.   Oh, yes, I thought about it—but never got any further. Every time I intended to set to work, it seemed just as if a hand held me back. Not to-day, I thought—to-morrow; and nothing ever came of it.

Hilda.   But why did you keep putting it off like that?

Solness.   Because I was revolving something in my mind. (*Slowly, and in a low voice.*) Through that little black crack in the chimney, I might, perhaps, force my way upwards—as a builder.

Hilda (looking straight in front of her).   That must have been thrilling.

Solness.   Almost irresistible—quite irresistible. For at that time it appeared to me a perfectly simple and straightforward matter. I would have had it happen in the wintertime—a little before midday. I was to be out driving Aline in the sleigh. The servants at home would have made huge fires in the stoves.

Hilda.   For, of course, it was to be bitterly cold that day?

Solness.   Rather biting, yes—and they would want Aline to find it thoroughly snug and warm when she came home.

Hilda.   I suppose she is very chilly by nature?

Solness.   She is. And as we drove home, we were to see the smoke.

Hilda.   Only the smoke?

Solness.   The smoke first. But when we came up to the garden gate, the whole of the old timber-box was to be a rolling mass of flames.— That is how I wanted it to be, you see.

Hilda.   Oh why, why could it not have happened so!

Solness.   You may well say that, Hilda.

Hilda. Well, but now listen, Mr. Solness. Are you perfectly certain that the fire was caused by that little crack in the chimney?

Solness. No, on the contrary—I am perfectly certain that the crack in the chimney had nothing whatever to do with the fire.

Hilda. What?

Solness. It has been clearly ascertained that the fire broke out in a clothes-cupboard—in a totally different part of the house.

Hilda. Then what is all this nonsense you are talking about the crack in the chimney?

Solness. May I go on talking to you a little, Hilda?

Hilda. Yes, if you'll only talk sensibly——

Solness. I will try.

[*He moves his chair nearer.*]

Hilda. Out with it, then, Mr. Solness.

Solness (confidentially). Don't you agree with me, Hilda, that there exist special, chosen people who have been endowed with the power and faculty of desiring a thing, craving for a thing, willing a thing—so persistently and so—so inexorably—that at last it has to happen? Don't you believe that?

Hilda (with an indefinable expression in her eyes). If that is so, we shall see, one of these days, whether I am one of the chosen.

Solness. It is not one's self alone that can do such great things. Oh, no—the helpers and the servers—they must do their part, too, if it is to be of any good. But they never come of themselves. One has to call upon them very persistently—inwardly, you understand.

Hilda. What are these helpers and servers?

Solness. Oh, we can talk about that some other time. For the present, let us keep to this business of the fire.

Hilda. Don't you think that fire would have happened all the same—even without your wishing for it?

Solness. If the house had been old Knut Brovik's, it would never have burnt down so conveniently for him. I am sure of that; for he does not know how to call for the helpers—no, nor for the servers, either. (*Rises in unrest.*) So you see, Hilda—it is my fault, after all, that the lives of the two little boys had to be sacrificed. And do you think it is not my fault, too, that Aline has never been the woman she should and might have been—and that she most longed to be?

Hilda. Yes, but if it is all the work of those helpers and servers——?

Solness. Who called for the helpers and servers? It was I! And they came and obeyed my will. (*In increasing excitement.*) That is what people call having the luck on your side; but I must tell you what this sort of luck feels like! It feels like a great raw place here on my breast.

And the helpers and servers keep on flaying pieces of skin off other people in order to close my sore!—But still the sore is not healed—never, never! Oh, if you knew how it can sometimes gnaw and burn.

Hilda (looks attentively at him). You are ill, Mr. Solness. Very ill, I almost think.

Solness. Say mad; for that is what you mean.

Hilda. No, I don't think there is much amiss with your intellect.

Solness. With what then? Out with it!

Hilda. I wonder whether you were not sent into the world with a sickly conscience.

Solness. A sickly conscience? What devilry is that?

Hilda. I mean that your conscience is feeble—too delicately built, as it were—hasn't strength to take a grip of things—to lift and bear what is heavy.

Solness (growls). H'm! May I ask, then, what sort of conscience one ought to have?

Hilda. I should like your conscience to be—to be thoroughly robust.

Solness. Indeed? Robust, eh? Is your own conscience robust, may I ask?

Hilda. Yes, I think it is. I have never noticed that it wasn't.

Solness. It has not been put very severely to the test, I should think.

Hilda (with a quivering of the lips). Oh, it was no such simple matter to leave father—I am so awfully fond of him.

Solness. Dear me! for a month or two——

Hilda. I think I shall never go home again.

Solness. Never? Then why did you leave him?

Hilda (half-seriously, half-banteringly). Have you forgotten that the ten years are up?

Solness. Oh nonsense. Was anything wrong at home? Eh?

Hilda (quite seriously). It was this impulse within me that urged and goaded me to come—and lured and drew me on, as well.

Solness (eagerly). There we have it! There we have it, Hilda! There is a troll in you, too, as in me. For it's the troll in one, you see—it is that that calls to the powers outside us. And then you must give in—whether you will or no.

Hilda. I almost think you are right, Mr. Solness.

Solness (walks about the room). Oh, there are devils innumerable abroad in the world, Hilda, that one never sees!

Hilda. Devils, too?

Solness (stops). Good devils and bad devils; light-haired devils and black-haired devils. If only you could always tell whether it is the light or dark ones that have got hold of you! (*Paces about.*) Ho-ho! Then it would be simple enough.

Hilda (follows him with her eyes). Or if one had a really vigorous, radiantly healthy conscience—so that one dared to do what one would.

Solness (stops beside the console table). I believe, now, that most people are just as puny creatures as I am in that respect.

Hilda. I shouldn't wonder.

Solness (leaning against the table). In the sagas—— Have you read any of the old sagas?

Hilda. Oh, yes! When I used to read books, I——

Solness. In the sagas you read about vikings, who sailed to foreign lands, and plundered and burned and killed men——

Hilda. And carried off women——

Solness. ——and kept them in captivity——

Hilda. ——took them home in their ships——

Solness. ——and behaved to them like—like the very worst of trolls.

Hilda (looks straight before her, with a half-veiled look). I think that must have been thrilling.

Solness (with a short, deep laugh). To carry off women,

Hilda. To be carried off.

Solness (looks at her a moment). Oh, indeed.

Hilda (as if breaking the thread of the conversation). But what made you speak of these vikings, Mr. Solness?

Solness. Why, those fellows must have had robust consciences, if you like! When they got home again, they could eat, and drink and be as happy as children. And the women, too! They often would not leave them on any account. Can you understand that, Hilda?

Hilda. Those women I can understand exceedingly well.

Solness. Oho! Perhaps you could do the same yourself?

Hilda. Why not?

Solness. Live—of your own free will—with a ruffian like that?

Hilda. If it was a ruffian I had come to love——

Solness. Could you come to love a man like that?

Hilda. Good heavens, you know very well one can't choose whom one is going to love.

Solness (looks meditatively at her). Oh, no, I suppose it is the troll within one that's responsible for that.

Hilda (half-laughing). And all those blessed devils, that you know so well—both the light-haired and the dark-haired ones.

Solness (quietly and warmly). Then I hope with all my heart that the devils will choose carefully for you, Hilda.

Hilda. For me they have chosen already—once and for all.

Solness (looks earnestly at her). Hilda—you are like a wild bird of the woods.

Hilda. Far from it. I don't hide myself away under the bushes.

Solness. No, no. There is rather something of the bird of prey in you.

Hilda. That is nearer it—perhaps. *(Very earnestly.)* And why not a bird of prey? Why should not *I* go a-hunting—I, as well as the rest. Carry off the prey I want—if only I can get my claws into it and do with it as I will.

Solness. Hilda—do you know what you are?

Hilda. Yes, I suppose I am a strange sort of bird.

Solness. No. You are like a dawning day. When I look at you—I seem to be looking towards the sunrise.

Hilda. Tell me, Mr. Solness—are you certain that you have never called me to you? Inwardly, you know?

Solness (softly and slowly). I almost think I must have.

Hilda. What did you want with me?

Solness. You are the younger generation, Hilda.

Hilda (smiles). That younger generation that you are so afraid of?

Solness (nods slowly). And which, in my heart, I yearn twards so deeply.

[HILDA *rises, goes to the little table and fetches* RAGNAR BROVIK's *portfolio.*]

Hilda (holds out the portfolio to him). We were talking of these drawings——

Solness (shortly, waving them away). Put those things away! I have seen enough of them.

Hilda. Yes, but you have to write your approval on them.

Solness. Write my approval on them? Never!

Hilda. But the poor old man is lying at death's door! Can't you give him and his son this pleasure before they are parted? And perhaps he might get the commission to carry them out, too.

Solness. Yes, that is just what he would get. He has made sure of that—has my fine gentleman!

Hilda. Then, good heavens—if that is so—can't you tell the least little bit of a lie for once in a way?

Solness. A lie? *(Raging.)* Hilda—take those devil's drawings out of my sight!

Hilda (draws the portfolio a little nearer to herself). Well, well, well—don't bite me.—You talk of trolls—but I think you go on like a troll yourself. *(Looks around.)* Where do you keep your pen and ink?

Solness. There is nothing of the sort in here.

Hilda (goes towards the door). But in the office where that young lady is——

Solness. Stay where you are, Hilda!—I ought to tell a lie, you say. Oh, yes, for the sake of his old father I might well do that—for in my time I have crushed him, trodden him under foot——

Hilda. Him, too?

Solness. I needed room for myself. But this Ragnar—he must on no account be allowed to come to the front.

Hilda. Poor fellow, there is surely no fear of that. If he has nothing in him——

Solness (comes closer, looks at her and whispers). If Ragnar Brovik gets his chance, he will strike me to the earth. Crush me—as I crushed his father.

Hilda. Crush you? Has he the ability for that?

Solness. Yes, you may depend upon it he has the ability! He is the younger generation that stands ready to knock at my door—to make an end of Halvard Solness.

Hilda (looks at him with quiet reproach). And yet you would bar him out. Fie, Mr. Solness!

Solness. The fight I have been fighting has cost heart's blood enough.—And I am afraid, too, that the helpers and servers will not obey me any longer.

Hilda. Then you must go ahead without them. There is nothing else for it.

Solness. It is hopeless, Hilda. The luck is bound to turn. A little sooner or a little later. Retribution is inexorable.

Hilda (in distress, putting her hands over her ears). Don't talk like that! Do you want to kill me? To take from me what is more than my life?

Solness. And what is that?

Hilda. The longing to see you great. To see you, with a wreath in your hand, high, high up upon a church-tower. *(Calm again.)* Come, out with your pencil now. You must have a pencil about you?

Solness (takes out his pocket-book). I have one here.

Hilda (lays the portfolio on the sofa-table). Very well. Now let us two sit down here, Mr. Solness. (SOLNESS *seats himself at the table.* HILDA *stands behind him, leaning over the back of the chair.)* And now we will write on the drawings. We must write very, very nicely and cordially—for this horrid Ruar—or whatever his name is.

Solness (writes a few words, turns his head and looks at her). Tell me one thing, Hilda.

Hilda. Yes!

Solness. If you have been waiting for me all these ten years——

Hilda. What then?

Solness. Why have you never written to me? Then I could have answered you.

Hilda (hastily). No, no, no! That was just what I did not want.

Solness. Why not?

Hilda. I was afraid the whole thing might fall to pieces.—But we were going to write on the drawings, Mr. Solness.

Solness. So we were.

Hilda (bends forward and looks over his shoulder while he writes). Mind now, kindly and cordially! Oh how I hate—how I hate this Ruald——

Solness (writing). Have you never really cared for any one, Hilda?

Hilda (harshly). What do you say?

Solness. Have you never cared for any one?

Hilda. For any one else, I suppose you mean?

Solness (looks up at her). For any one else, yes. Have you never? In all these ten years? Never?

Hilda. Oh, yes, now and then. When I was perfectly furious with you for not coming.

Solness. Then you did take an interest in other people, too?

Hilda. A little bit—for a week or so. Good heavens, Mr. Solness, you surely know how such things come about.

Solness. Hilda—what is it you have come for?

Hilda. Don't waste time talking. The poor old man might go and die in the meantime.

Solness. Answer me, Hilda. What do you want of me?

Hilda. I want my kingdom.

Solness. H'm——

[*He gives a rapid glance towards the door on the left and then goes on writing on the drawings. At the same moment* MRS. SOLNESS *enters; she has some packages in her hand.*]

Mrs. Solness. Here are a few things I have got for you, Miss Wangel. The large parcels will be sent later on.

Hilda. Oh, how very, very kind of you!

Mrs. Solness. Only my simple duty. Nothing more than that.

Solness (reading over what he has written). Aline!

Mrs. Solness. Yes?

Solness. Did you notice whether the—the book-keeper was out there?

Mrs. Solness. Yes, of course, she was out there.

Solness (puts the drawings in the portfolio). H'm——

Mrs. Solness. She was standing at the desk, as she always is—when I go through the room.

Solness (rises). Then I'll give this to her and tell her that——

Hilda (takes the portfolio from him). Oh, no, let me have the pleasure of doing that! (*Goes to the door, but turns.*) What is her name?

Solness.   Her name is Miss Fosli.

Hilda.   Pooh, that sounds too cold! Her Christian name, I mean?

Solness.   Kaia—I believe.

Hilda (opens the door and calls out).   Kaia, come in here! Make haste! Mr. Solness wants to speak to you.

[KAIA FOSLI *appears at the door.*]

Kaia (looking at him in alarm).   Here I am——?

Hilda (handing her the portfolio).   See here, Kaia! You can take this home; Mr. Solness has written on them now.

Kaia.   Oh, at last!

Solness.   Give them to the old man as soon as you can.

Kaia.   I will go straight home with them.

Solness.   Yes, do. Now Ragnar will have a chance of building for himself.

Kaia.   Oh, may he come and thank you for all——?

Solness (harshly).   I won't have any thanks! Tell him that from me.

Kaia.   Yes, I will——

Solness.   And tell him at the same time that henceforward I do not require his services—nor yours either.

Kaia (softly and quiveringly).   Not mine either?

Solness.   You will have other things to think of now and to attend to; and that is a very good thing for you. Well, go home with the drawings now, Miss Fosli. At once! Do you hear?

Kaia (as before).   Yes, Mr. Solness.

[*She goes out.*]

Mrs. Solness.   Heavens! what deceitful eyes she has.

Solness.   She? That poor little creature?

Mrs. Solness.   Oh—I can see what I can see, Halvard.—— Are you really dismissing them?

Solness.   Yes.

Mrs. Solness.   Her as well?

Solness.   Was not that what you wished?

Mrs. Solness.   But how can you get on without her——? Oh, well, no doubt you have some one else in reserve, Halvard.

Hilda (playfully).   Well, I for one am not the person to stand at that desk.

Solness.   Never mind, never mind—it will be all right, Aline. Now all you have to do is to think about moving into our new home—as quickly as you can. This evening we will hang up the wreath—*(Turns to* HILDA.*)*—right on the very pinnacle of the tower. What do you say to that, Miss Hilda?

Hilda (looks at him with sparkling eyes). It will be splendid to see you so high up once more.

Solness. Me!

Mrs. Solness. For heaven's sake, Miss Wangel, don't imagine such a thing! My husband!—when he always gets so dizzy!

Hilda. He get dizzy! No, I know quite well he does not!

Mrs. Solness. Oh, yes, indeed he does.

Hilda. But I have seen him with my own eyes right up at the top of a high church-tower!

Mrs. Solness. Yes, I hear people talk of that; but it is utterly impossible——

Solness (vehemently). Impossible—impossible, yes! But there I stood all the same!

Mrs. Solness. Oh, how can you say so, Halvard? Why, you can't even bear to go out on the second-story balcony here. You have always been like that.

Solness. You may perhaps see something different this evening.

Mrs. Solness (in alarm). No, no, no! Please God I shall never see that. I will write at once to the doctor—and I am sure he won't let you do it.

Solness. Why, Aline——!

Mrs. Solness. Oh, you know you're ill, Halvard. This proves it! Oh God—Oh God!

[*She goes hastily out to the right.*]

Hilda (looks intently at him). Is it so, or is it not?

Solness. That I turn dizzy?

Hilda. That my master builder dares not—cannot—climb as high as he builds?

Solness. Is that the way you look at it?

Hilda. Yes.

Solness. I believe there is scarcely a corner in me that is safe from you.

Hilda (looks towards the bow-window). Up there, then. Right up there——

Solness (approaches her). You might have the topmost room in the tower, Hilda—there you might live like a princess.

Hilda (indefinably, between earnest and jest). Yes, that is what you promised me.

Solness. Did I really?

Hilda. Fie, Mr. Solness! You said I should be a princess, and that you would give me a kingdom. And then you went and—— Well!

Solness (cautiously). Are you quite certain that this is not a dream—a fancy, that has fixed itself in your mind?

Hilda (sharply). Do you mean that you did not do it?

Solness. I scarcely know myself. *(More softly.)* But now I know so much for certain, that I——

Hilda. That you——? Say it at once!

Solness. —that I ought to have done it.

Hilda (exclaims with animation). Don't tell me you can ever be dizzy!

Solness. This evening, then, we will hang up the wreath—Princess Hilda.

Hilda (with a bitter curve of the lips). Over your new home, yes.

Solness. Over the new house, which will never be a home for me.

[*He goes out through the garden door.*]

Hilda (looks straight in front of her with a far-away expression and whispers to herself. The only words audible are) —frightfully thrilling——

ACT III

The large, broad verandah of SOLNESS's *dwelling-house. Part of the house, with outer door leading to the verandah, is seen to the left. A railing along the verandah to the right. At the back, from the end of the verandah, a flight of steps leads down to the garden below. Tall old trees in the garden spread their branches over the verandah and towards the house. Far to the right, in among the trees, a glimpse is caught of the lower part of the new villa, with scaffolding round so much as is seen of the tower. In the background the garden is bounded by an old wooden fence. Outside the fence, a street with low, tumble-down cottages.*

Evening sky with sun-lit clouds.

On the verandah, a garden bench stands along the wall of the house, and in front of the bench a long table. On the other side of the table, an arm-chair and some stools. All the furniture is of wicker-work.

MRS. SOLNESS, *wrapped in a large white crape shawl, sits resting in the arm-chair and gazes over to the right. Shortly after,* HILDA WANGEL *comes up the flight of steps from the garden. She is dressed as in the last act and wears her hat. She has in her bodice a little nosegay of small common flowers.*

    Mrs. Solness (turning her head a little). Have you been round the garden, Miss Wangel?

    Hilda. Yes, I have been taking a look at it.

    Mrs. Solness. And found some flowers, too, I see.

    Hilda. Yes, indeed! There are such heaps of them in among the bushes.

    Mrs. Solness. Are there really? Still? You see I scarcely ever go there.

    Hilda (closer). What! Don't you take a run down into the garden every day, then?

Mrs. Solness (with a faint smile). I don't "run" anywhere, nowadays.

Hilda. Well, but do you not go down now and then to look at all the lovely things there?

Mrs. Solness. It has all become so strange to me. I am almost afraid to see it again.

Hilda. Your own garden!

Mrs. Solness. I don't feel that it is mine any longer.

Hilda. What do you mean——?

Mrs. Solness. No, no, it is not—not—not as it was in my mother's and father's time. They have taken away so much—so much of the garden, Miss Wangel. Fancy—they have parcelled it out—and built houses for strangers—people that I don't know. And they can sit and look in upon me from their windows.

Hilda (with a bright expression). Mrs. Solness!

Mrs. Solness. Yes!

Hilda. May I stay here with you a little?

Mrs. Solness. Yes, by all means, if you care to.

[HILDA *moves a stool close to the arm-chair and sits down.*]

Hilda. Ah—here one can sit and sun oneself like a cat.

Mrs. Solness (lays her hand softly on HILDA'S *neck).* It is nice of you to be willing to sit with me. I thought you wanted to go in to my husband.

Hilda. What should I want with him?

Mrs. Solness. To help him, I thought.

Hilda. No, thank you. And besides, he is not in. He is over there with the workmen. But he looked so fierce that I did not care to talk to him.

Mrs. Solness. He is so kind and gentle in reality.

Hilda. He!

Mrs. Solness. You do not really know him yet, Miss Wangel.

Hilda (looks affectionately at her). Are you pleased at the thought of moving over to the new house?

Mrs. Solness. I ought to be pleased; for it is what Halvard wants——

Hilda. Oh, not just on that account, surely.

Mrs. Solness. Yes, yes, Miss Wangel; for it is only my duty to submit myself to him. But very often it is dreadfully difficult to force one's mind to obedience.

Hilda. Yes, that must be difficult indeed.

Mrs. Solness. I can tell you it is—when one has so many faults as I have——

Hilda. When one has gone through so much trouble as you have——

Mrs. Solness.   How do you know about that?

Hilda.   Your husband told me.

Mrs. Solness.   To me he very seldom mentions these things.——Yes, I can tell you I have gone through more than enough trouble in my life, Miss Wangel.

Hilda (looks sympathetically at her and nods slowly).   Poor Mrs. Solness. First of all there was the fire——

Mrs. Solness (with a sigh).   Yes, everything that was mine was burnt.

Hilda.   And then came what was worse.

Mrs. Solness (looking inquiringly at her).   Worse?

Hilda.   The worst of all.

Mrs. Solness.   What do you mean?

Hilda (softly).   You lost the two little boys.

Mrs. Solness.   Oh, yes, the boys. But, you see, that was a thing apart. That was a dispensation of Providence; and in such things one can only bow in submission—yes, and be thankful, too.

Hilda.   Then you are so?

Mrs. Solness.   Not always, I am sorry to say. I know well enough that it is my duty—but all the same I cannot.

Hilda.   No, no, I think that is only natural.

Mrs. Solness.   And often and often I have to remind myself that it was a righteous punishment for me——

Hilda.   Why?

Mrs. Solness.   Because I had not fortitude enough in misfortune.

Hilda.   But I don't see that——

Mrs. Solness.   Oh, no, no, Miss Wangel—do not talk to me any more about the two little boys. We ought to feel nothing but joy in thinking of them; for they are so happy—so happy now. No, it is the small losses in life that cut one to the heart—the loss of all that other people look upon as almost nothing.

Hilda (lays her arms on MRS. SOLNESS's *knees and looks up at her affectionately).*   Dear Mrs. Solness—tell me what things you mean!

Mrs. Solness.   As I say, only little things. All the old portraits were burnt on the walls. And all the old silk dresses were burnt, that had belonged to the family for generations and generations. And all mother's and grandmother's lace—that was burnt, too. And only think—the jewels, too! (*Sadly.*) And then all the dolls.

Hilda.   The dolls?

Mrs. Solness (choking with tears).   I had nine lovely dolls.

Hilda.   And they were burnt, too?

Mrs. Solness.   All of them. Oh, it was hard—so hard for me.

Hilda.   Had you put by all these dolls, then? Ever since you were little?

Mrs. Solness. I had not put them by. The dolls and I had gone on living together.

Hilda. After you were grown up?

Mrs. Solness. Yes, long after that.

Hilda. After you were married, too?

Mrs. Solness. Oh, yes, indeed. So long as he did not see it——. But they were all burnt up, poor things. No one thought of saving them. Oh, it is so miserable to think of. You mustn't laugh at me, Miss Wangel.

Hilda. I am not laughing at the least.

Mrs. Solness. For you see, in a certain sense, there was life in them, too. I carried them under my heart—like little unborn children.

[DR. HERDAL, *with his hat in his hand, comes out through the door and observes* MRS. SOLNESS *and* HILDA.]

Dr. Herdal. Well, Mrs. Solness, so you are sitting out here catching cold?

Mrs. Solness. I find it so pleasant and warm here to-day.

Dr. Herdal. Yes, yes. But is there anything going on here? I got a note from you.

Mrs. Solness (rises). Yes, there is something I must talk to you about.

Dr. Herdal. Very well; then perhaps we had better go in. *(To* HILDA.) Still in your mountaineering dress, Miss Wangel?

Hilda (gaily, rising). Yes—in full uniform! But to-day I am not going climbing and breaking my neck. We two will stop quietly below and look on, doctor.

Dr. Herdal. What are we to look on at?

Mrs. Solness (softly, in alarm, to HILDA). Hush, hush—for God's sake! He is coming. Try to get that idea out of his head. And let us be friends, Miss Wangel. Don't you think we can?

Hilda (throws her arms impetuously round MRS. SOLNESS's *neck).* Oh, if we only could!

Mrs. Solness (gently disengages herself). There, there, there! There he comes, doctor. Let me have a word with you.

Dr. Herdal. Is it about him?

Mrs. Solness. Yes, to be sure it's about him. Do come in.

[*She and the doctor enter the house. Next moment* SOLNESS *comes up from the garden by the flight of steps. A serious look comes over* HILDA's *face.*]

Solness (glances at the house-door, which is closed cautiously from within). Have you noticed, Hilda, that as soon as I come, she goes?

Hilda.   I have noticed that as soon as you come, you make her go.

Solness.   Perhaps so. But I cannot help it. (*Looks observantly at her.*) Are you cold, Hilda? I think you look cold.

Hilda.   I have just come up out of a tomb.

Solness.   What do you mean by that?

Hilda.   That I have got chilled through and through, Mr. Solness.

Solness (slowly).   I believe I understand——

Hilda.   What brings you up here just now?

Solness.   I caught sight of you from over there.

Hilda.   But then you must have seen her too?

Solness.   I knew she would go at once if I came.

Hilda.   Is it very painful for you that she should avoid you in this way?

Solness.   In one sense, it's a relief as well.

Hilda.   Not to have her before your eyes?

Solness.   Yes.

Hilda.   Not to be always seeing how heavily the loss of the little boys weighs upon her?

Solness.   Yes. Chiefly that.

[HILDA *drifts across the verandah with her hands behind her back, stops at the railing and looks out over the garden.*]

Solness (after a short pause).   Did you have a long talk with her?

[HILDA *stands motionless and does not answer.*]

Solness.   Had you a long talk, I asked?

[HILDA *is silent as before.*]

Solness.   What was she talking about, Hilda?

[HILDA *continues silent.*]

Solness.   Poor Aline! I suppose it was about the little boys.

Hilda (a nervous shudder runs through her; then she nods hurriedly once or twice).

Solness.   She will never get over it—never in this world. (*Approaches her.*) Now you are standing there again like a statue; just as you stood last night.

Hilda (turns and looks at him, with great serious eyes).   I am going away.

Solness (sharply).   Going away!

Hilda.   Yes.

Solness.   But I won't allow you to!

Hilda.   What am I to do here now?

Solness.   Simply to be here, Hilda!

Hilda (measures him with a look).   Oh, thank you. You know it wouldn't end there.

Solness (heedlessly).   So much the better!

Hilda (vehemently).   I cannot do any harm to one whom I know! I can't take away anything that belongs to her.

Solness.   Who wants you to do that?

Hilda (continuing).   A stranger, yes! for that is quite a different thing! A person I have never set eyes on. But one that I have come into close contact with——! Oh, no! Oh, no! Ugh!

Solness.   Yes, but I never proposed you should.

Hilda.   Oh, Mr. Solness, you know quite well what the end of it would be. And that is why I am going away.

Solness.   And what is to become of me when you are gone? What shall I have to live for then?—After that?

Hilda (with the indefinable look in her eyes).   It is surely not so hard for you. You have your duties to her. Live for those duties.

Solness.   Too late. These powers—these—these——

Hilda.   —devils——

Solness.   Yes, these devils! And the troll within me as well—they have drawn all the life-blood out of her. *(Laughs in desperation.)* They did it for my happiness! Yes, yes! *(Sadly.)* And now she is dead—for my sake. And I am chained alive to a dead woman. *(In wild anguish.)* I—I who cannot live without joy in life!

[HILDA *moves round the table and seats herself on the bench, with her elbows on the table, and her head supported by her hands.*]

Hilda (sits and looks at him awhile).   What will you build next?

Solness (shakes his head).   I don't believe I shall build much more.

Hilda.   Not those cosy, happy homes for mother and father, and for the troop of children?

Solness.   I wonder whether there will be any use for such homes in the coming time.

Hilda.   Poor Mr. Solness! And you have gone all these ten years—and staked your whole life—on that alone.

Solness.   Yes, you may well say so, Hilda.

Hilda (with an outburst).   Oh, it all seems to me so foolish—so foolish!

Solness.   All what?

Hilda.   Not to be able to grasp at your own happiness—at your own life! Merely because some one you know happens to stand in the way!

Solness.   One whom you have no right to set aside.

Hilda. I wonder whether one really has not the right! And yet, and yet——. Oh, if one could only sleep the whole thing away!

[*She lays her arms flat on the table, rests the left side of her head on her hands and shuts her eyes.*]

Solness (turns the arm-chair and sits down at the table). Had you a cosy, happy home—up there with your father, Hilda?

Hilda (without stirring, answers as if half asleep). I had only a cage.

Solness. And you are determined not to go back to it?

Hilda (as before). The wild bird never wants to go into the cage.

Solness. Rather range through the free air——

Hilda (still as before). The bird of prey loves to range——

Solness (lets his eyes rest on her). If only one had the viking-spirit in life——

Hilda (in her usual voice; opens her eyes but does not move). And the other thing? Say what that was!

Solness. A robust conscience.

[HILDA *sits erect on the bench, with animation. Her eyes have once more the sparkling expression of gladness.*]

Hilda (nods to him). I know what you are going to build next!

Solness. Then you know more than I do, Hilda.

Hilda. Yes, builders are such stupid people.

Solness. What is it to be then?

Hilda (nods again). The castle.

Solness. What castle?

Hilda. My castle, of course.

Solness. Do you want a castle now?

Hilda. Don't you owe me a kingdom, I should like to know?

Solness. You say I do.

Hilda. Well—you admit you owe me this kingdom. And you can't have a kingdom without a royal castle, I should think!

Solness (more and more animated). Yes, they usually go together.

Hilda. Good! Then build it for me! This moment!

Solness (laughing). Must you have that on the instant, too?

Hilda. Yes, to be sure! For the ten years are up now, and I am not going to wait any longer. So—out with the castle, Mr. Solness!

Solness. It's no light matter to owe you anything, Hilda.

Hilda. You should have thought of that before. It is too late now. So—(*tapping the table*)—the castle on the table! It is my castle! I will have it at once!

Solness (more seriously, leans over towards her, with his arms on the table). What sort of castle have you imagined, Hilda?

[*Her expression becomes more and more veiled. She seems gazing inwards at herself.*]

Hilda (slowly). My castle shall stand on a height—on a very great height—with a clear outlook on all sides, so that I can see far—far around.

Solness. And no doubt it is to have a high tower!

Hilda. A tremendously high tower. And at the very top of the tower there shall be a balcony. And I will stand out upon it——

Solness (involuntarily clutches at his forehead). How can you like to stand at such a dizzy height——?

Hilda. Yes, I will, right up there will I stand and look down on the other people—on those that are building churches, and homes for mother and father and the troop of children. And you may come up and look on at it, too.

Solness (in a low tone). Is the builder to be allowed to come up beside the princess?

Hilda. If the builder will.

Solness (more softly). Then I think the builder will come.

Hilda (nods). The builder—he will come.

Solness. But he will never be able to build any more. Poor builder!

Hilda (animated). Oh yes, he will! We two will set to work together. And then we will build the loveliest—the very loveliest—thing in all the world.

Solness (intently). Hilda—tell me what that is!

Hilda (looks smilingly at him, shakes her head a little, pouts and speaks as if to a child). Builders—they are such very—very stupid people.

Solness. Yes, no doubt they are stupid. But now tell me what it is—the loveliest thing in the world—that we two are to build together?

Hilda (is silent a little while, then says with an indefinable expression in her eyes). Castles in the air.

Solness. Castles in the air?

Hilda (nods). Castles in the air, yes! Do you know what sort of thing a castle in the air is?

Solness. It is the loveliest thing in the world, you say.

Hilda (rises with vehemence and makes a gesture of repulsion with her hand). Yes, to be sure it is! Castles in the air—they are so easy to take refuge in. And so easy to build, too—(*looks scornfully at him*)—especially for the builders who have a—a dizzy conscience.

Solness (rises). After this day we two will build together, Hilda.

Hilda (with a half-dubious smile). A real castle in the air?

Solness. Yes. One with a firm foundation under it.

[RAGNAR BROVIK *comes out from the house. He is carrying a large, green wreath with flowers and silk ribbons.*]

Hilda (with an outburst of pleasure).   The wreath! Oh, that will be glorious!

Solness (in surprise).   Have you brought the wreath, Ragnar?

Ragnar.   I promised the foreman I would.

Solness (relieved).   Ah, then I suppose your father is better?

Ragnar.   No.

Solness.   Was he not cheered by what I wrote?

Ragnar.   It came too late.

Solness.   Too late!

Ragnar.   When she came with it he was unconscious. He had had a stroke.

Solness.   Why, then, you must go home to him! You must attend to your father!

Ragnar.   He does not need me any more.

Solness.   But surely you ought to be with him.

Ragnar.   She is sitting by his bed.

Solness (rather uncertainly).   Kaia?

Ragnar (looking darkly at him).   Yes—Kaia.

Solness.   Go home, Ragnar—both to him and to her. Give me the wreath.

Ragnar (suppresses a mocking smile).   You don't mean that you yourself——?

Solness.   I will take it down to them myself. (*Takes the wreath from him.*) And now you go home; we don't require you to-day.

Ragnar.   I know you do not require me any more; but to-day I shall remain.

Solness.   Well, remain then, since you are bent upon it.

Hilda (at the railing).   Mr. Solness, I will stand here and look on at you.

Solness.   At me!

Hilda.   It will be fearfully thrilling.

Solness (in a low tone).   We will talk about that presently, Hilda.

[*He goes down the flight of steps with the wreath and away through the garden.*]

Hilda (looks after him, then turns to RAGNAR).   I think you might at least have thanked him.

Ragnar.   Thanked him? Ought I to have thanked him?

Hilda.   Yes, of course you ought!

Ragnar.   I think it is rather you I ought to thank.

Hilda. How can you say such a thing?

Ragnar (without answering her). But I advise you to take care, Miss Wangel! For you don't know him rightly yet.

Hilda (ardently). Oh, no one knows him as I do!

Ragnar (laughs in exasperation). Thank him, when he has held me down year after year! When he made father disbelieve in me—made me disbelieve in myself! And all merely that he might——!

Hilda (as if divining something). That he might——? Tell me at once!

Ragnar. That he might keep her with him.

Hilda (with a start towards him). The girl at the desk.

Ragnar. Yes.

Hilda (threateningly, clenching her hands). That is not true! You are telling falsehoods about him!

Ragnar. I would not believe it either until to-day—when she said so herself.

Hilda (as if beside herself). What did she say? I will know! At once! at once!

Ragnar. She said that he had taken possession of her mind—her whole mind—centred all her thoughts upon himself alone. She says that she can never leave him—that she will remain here, where he is——

Hilda (with flashing eyes). She will not be allowed to!

Ragnar (as if feeling his way). Who will not allow her?

Hilda (rapidly). He will not either!

Ragnar. Oh no—I understand the whole thing now. After this, she would merely be—in the way.

Hilda. You understand nothing—since you can talk like that! No, I will tell you why he kept hold of her.

Ragnar. Well then, why?

Hilda. In order to keep hold of you.

Ragnar. Has he told you so?

Hilda. No, but it is so. It must be so! *(Wildly.)* I will—I will have it so!

Ragnar. And at the very moment when you came—he let her go.

Hilda. It was you—you that he let go. What do you suppose he cares about strange women like her?

Ragnar (reflects). Is it possible that all this time he has been afraid of me?

Hilda. He afraid! I would not be so conceited if I were you.

Ragnar. Oh, he must have seen long ago that I had something in me, too. Besides—cowardly—that is just what he is, you see.

Hilda. He! Oh, yes, I am likely to believe that!

Ragnar. In a certain sense he is cowardly—he, the great master builder. He is not afraid of robbing others of their life's happiness—as he has done both for my father and for me. But when it comes to climbing up a paltry bit of scaffolding—he will do anything rather than that.

Hilda. Oh, you should just have seen him high, high up—at the dizzy height where I once saw him.

Ragnar. Did you see that?

Hilda. Yes, indeed I did. How free and great he looked as he stood and fastened the wreath to the church-vane!

Ragnar. I know that he ventured that, once in his life—one solitary time. It is a legend among us younger men. But no power on earth would induce him to do it again.

Hilda. To-day he will do it again!

Ragnar (scornfully). Yes, I daresay!

Hilda. We shall see it!

Ragnar. That neither you nor I will see.

Hilda (with uncontrollable vehemence). I will see it! I will and must see it!

Ragnar. But he will not do it. He simply dare not do it. For you see he cannot get over this infirmity—master builder though he be.

[MRS. SOLNESS *comes from the house on to the verandah.*]

Mrs. Solness (looks around). Is he not here? Where has he gone to?

Ragnar. Mr. Solness is down with the men.

Hilda. He took the wreath with him.

Mrs. Solness (terrified). Took the wreath with him! Oh, God! oh, God! Brovik—you must go down to him! Get him to come back here!

Ragnar. Shall I say you want to speak to him, Mrs. Solness?

Mrs. Solness. Oh, yes, do!—No, no—don't say that *I* want anything! You can say that somebody is here, and that he must come at once.

Ragnar. Good. I will do so, Mrs. Solness.

[*He goes down the flight of steps and away through the garden.*]

Mrs. Solness. Oh, Miss Wangel, you can't think how anxious I feel about him.

Hilda. Is there anything in this to be so terribly frightened about?

Mrs. Solness. Oh, yes; surely you can understand. Just think, if he were really to do it! If he should take it into his head to climb up the scaffolding!

Hilda (eagerly). Do you think he will?

Mrs. Solness.   Oh, one can never tell what he might take into his head. I am afraid there is nothing he mightn't think of doing.

Hilda.   Aha! Perhaps you too think that he is—well——?

Mrs. Solness.   Oh, I don't know what to think about him now. The doctor has been telling me all sorts of things; and putting it all together with several things I have heard him say——

[DR. HERDAL *looks out, at the door.*]

Dr. Herdal.   Is he not coming soon?

Mrs. Solness.   Yes, I think so. I have sent for him at any rate.

Dr. Herdal (advancing).   I am afraid you will have to go in, my dear lady——

Mrs. Solness.   Oh, no! Oh, no! I shall stay out here and wait for Halvard.

Dr. Herdal.   But some ladies have just come to call on you——

Mrs. Solness.   Good heavens, that too! And just at this moment!

Dr. Herdal.   They say they positively must see the ceremony.

Mrs. Solness.   Well, well, I suppose I must go to them after all. It is my duty.

Hilda.   Can't you ask the ladies to go away?

Mrs. Solness.   No, that would never do. Now that they are here, it is my duty to see them. But do you stay out here in the meantime—and receive him when he comes.

Dr. Herdal.   And try to occupy his attention as long as possible——

Mrs. Solness.   Yes, do, dear Miss Wangel. Keep a firm hold of him as ever you can.

Hilda.   Would it not be best for you to do that?

Mrs. Solness.   Yes; God knows that is my duty. But when one has duties in so many directions——

Dr. Herdal (looks towards the garden).   There he is coming.

Mrs. Solness.   And I have to go in!

Dr. Herdal (to HILDA).   Don't say anything about my being here.

Hilda.   Oh, no! I daresay I shall find something else to talk to Mr. Solness about.

Mrs. Solness.   And be sure you keep firm hold of him. I believe you can do it best.

[MRS. SOLNESS *and* DR. HERDAL *go into the house.* HILDA *remains standing on the verandah.* SOLNESS *comes from the garden, up the flight of steps.*]

Solness.   Somebody wants me, I hear.

Hilda.   Yes; it is I, Mr. Solness.

Solness. Oh, is it you, Hilda? I was afraid it might be Aline or the Doctor.

Hilda. You are very easily frightened, it seems!

Solness. Do you think so?

Hilda. Yes; people say that you are afraid to climb about—on the scaffoldings, you know.

Solness. Well, that is quite a special thing.

Hilda. Then it is true that you are afraid to do it?

Solness. Yes, I am.

Hilda. Afraid of falling down and killing yourself?

Solness. No, not of that.

Hilda. Of what, then?

Solness. I am afraid of retribution, Hilda.

Hilda. Of retribution? *(Shakes her head.)* I don't understand that.

Solness. Sit down and I will tell you something.

Hilda. Yes, do! At once!

[*She sits on a stool by the railing and looks expectantly at him.*]

Solness (throws his hat on the table). You know that I began by building churches.

Hilda (nods). I know that well.

Solness. For, you see, I came as a boy from a pious home in the country; and so it seemed to me that this church-building was the noblest task I could set myself.

Hilda. Yes, yes.

Solness. And I venture to say that I built those poor little churches with such honest and warm and heartfelt devotion that—that——

Hilda. That——? Well?

Solness. Well, that I think that he ought to have been pleased with me.

Hilda. He? What he?

Solness. He who was to have the churches, of course! He to whose honour and glory they were dedicated.

Hilda. Oh, indeed! But are you certain, then, that—that he was not—pleased with you?

Solness (scornfully). He pleased with me! How can you talk so, Hilda? He who gave the troll in me leave to lord it just as it pleased. He who bade them be at hand to serve me, both day and night—all these—all these——

Hilda. Devils——

Solness. Yes, of both kinds. Oh, no, he made me feel clearly enough that he was not pleased with me. *(Mysteriously.)* You see, that was really the reason why he made the old house burn down.

Hilda. Was that why?

Solness. Yes, don't you understand? He wanted to give me the chance of becoming an accomplished master in my own sphere—so that I might build all the more glorious churches for him. At first I did not understand what he was driving at; but all of a sudden it flashed upon me.

Hilda. When was that?

Solness. It was when I was building the church-tower up at Lysanger.

Hilda. I thought so.

Solness. For you see, Hilda—up there, amidst those new surroundings, I used to go about musing and pondering within myself. Then I saw plainly why he had taken my little children from me. It was that I should have nothing else to attach myself to. No such thing as love and happiness, you understand. I was to be only a master builder—nothing else. And all my life long I was to go on building for him. *(Laughs.)* But I can tell you nothing came of that!

Hilda. What did you do, then?

Solness. First of all, I searched and tried my own heart——

Hilda. And then?

Solness. Then I did the impossible—I no less than he.

Hilda. The impossible?

Solness. I had never before been able to climb up to a great, free height. But that day I did it.

Hilda (leaping up). Yes, yes, you did!

Solness. And when I stood there, high over everything, and was hanging the wreath over the vane, I said to him: Hear me now, thou Mighty One! From this day forward I will be a free builder—I, too, in my sphere—just as thou in thine. I will never more build churches for thee—only homes for human beings.

Hilda (with great sparkling eyes). That was the song that I heard through the air!

Solness. But afterwards his turn came.

Hilda. What do you mean by that?

Solness (looks despondently at her). Building homes for human beings—is not worth a rap, Hilda.

Hilda. Do you say that now?

Solness. Yes, for now I see it. Men have no use for these homes of theirs—to be happy in. And I should not have had any use for such a home, if I had had one. *(With a quiet, bitter laugh.)* See, that is the upshot of the whole affair, however far back I look. Nothing really built; nor anything sacrificed for the chance of building. Nothing, nothing! the whole is nothing.

Hilda. Then you will never build anything more?

Solness (with animation). On the contrary, I am just going to begin!

Hilda. What, then? What will you build? Tell me at once!

Solness. I believe there is only one possible dwelling-place for human happiness—and that is what I am going to build now.

Hilda (looks fixedly at him). Mr. Solness—you mean our castle?

Solness. The castles in the air—yes.

Hilda. I am afraid you would turn dizzy before we got half-way up.

Solness. Not if I can mount hand in hand with you, Hilda.

Hilda (with an expression of suppressed resentment). Only with me? Will there be no others of the party?

Solness. Who else should there be?

Hilda. Oh—that girl—that Kaia at the desk. Poor thing—don't you want to take her with you, too?

Solness. Oho! Was it about her that Aline was talking to you?

Hilda. Is it so—or is it not?

Solness (vehemently). I will not answer such a question. You must believe in me, wholly and entirely!

Hilda. All these ten years I have believed in you so utterly—so utterly.

Solness. You must go on believing in me!

Hilda. Then let me see you stand free and high up!

Solness (sadly). Oh Hilda—it is not every day that I can do that.

Hilda (passionately). I will have you do it! I will have it! (*Imploringly.*) Just once more, Mr. Solness! Do the impossible once again!

Solness (stands and looks deep into her eyes). If I try it, Hilda, I will stand up there and talk to him as I did that time before.

Hilda (in rising excitement). What will you say to him?

Solness. I will say to him: Hear me, Mighty Lord—thou may'st judge me as seems best to thee. But hereafter I will build nothing but the loveliest thing in the world——

Hilda (carried away). Yes—yes—yes!

Solness. —build it together with a princess, whom I love——

Hilda. Yes, tell him that! Tell him that!

Solness. Yes. And then I will say to him: Now I shall go down and throw my arms round her and kiss her——

Hilda. —many times! Say that!

Solness. —many, many times, I will say.

Hilda. And then——?

Solness. Then I will wave my hat—and come down to the earth—and do as I said to him.

Hilda (with outstretched arms). Now I see you again as I did when
there was song in the air.

Solness (looks at her with his head bowed). How have you become
what you are, Hilda?

Hilda. How have you made me what I am?

Solness (shortly and firmly). The princess shall have her castle.

Hilda (jubilant, clapping her hands). Oh, Mr. Solness——! My
lovely, lovely castle. Our castle in the air!

Solness. On a firm foundation.

> [*In the street a crowd of people has assembled, vaguely seen through
> the trees. Music of wind-instruments is heard far away behind the
> new house. MRS. SOLNESS, with a fur collar round her neck,
> DOCTOR HERDAL with her white shawl on his arm, and some
> ladies, come out on the verandah. RAGNAR BROVIK comes at the
> same time up from the garden.*]

Mrs. Solness (to RAGNAR). Are we to have music, too?

Ragnar. Yes. It's the band of the Mason's Union. *(To SOLNESS.)*
The foreman asked me to tell you that he is ready now to go up with
the wreath.

Solness (takes his hat). Good. I will go down to him myself.

Mrs. Solness (anxiously). What have you to do down there,
Halvard?

Solness (curtly). I must be down below with the men.

Mrs. Solness. Yes, down below—only down below.

Solness. That is where I always stand—on everyday occasions.

> [*He goes down the flight of steps and away through the garden.*]

Mrs. Solness (calls after him over the railing). But do beg the man
to be careful when he goes up? Promise me that, Halvard!

Dr. Herdal (to MRS. SOLNESS). Don't you see that I was right? He
has given up all thought of that folly.

Mrs. Solness. Oh, what a relief! Twice workmen have fallen, and
each time they were killed on the spot. *(Turns to HILDA.)* Thank you,
Miss Wangel, for having kept such a firm hold upon him. I should
never have been able to manage him.

Dr. Herdal (playfully). Yes, yes, Miss Wangel, you know how to
keep firm hold on a man, when you give your mind to it.

> [MRS. SOLNESS *and* DR. HERDAL *go up to the ladies, who are
> standing nearer to the steps and looking over the garden.* HILDA
> *remains standing beside the railing in the foreground.* RAGNAR
> *goes up to her.*]

Ragnar (with suppressed laughter, half whispering).   Miss Wangel—
do you see all those young fellows down in the street?

Hilda.   Yes.

Ragnar.   They are my fellow-students, come to look at the master.

Hilda.   What do they want to look at him for?

Ragnar.   They want to see how he daren't climb to the top of his
own house.

Hilda.   Oh, that is what those boys want, is it?

Ragnar (spitefully and scornfully).   He has kept us down so long—
now we are going to see him keep quietly down below himself.

Hilda.   You will not see that—not this time.

Ragnar (smiles).   Indeed! Then where shall we see him?

Hilda.   High—high up by the vane! That is where you will see him!

Ragnar (laughs).   Him! Oh, yes, I daresay!

Hilda.   His will is to reach the top—so at the top you shall see him.

Ragnar.   His will, yes; that I can easily believe. But he simply cannot do it. His head would swim round, long, long before he got half-
way. He would have to crawl down again on his hands and knees.

Dr. Herdal (points across).   Look! There goes the foreman up the
ladders.

Mrs. Solness.   And of course he has the wreath to carry, too. Oh, I
do hope he will be careful!

Ragnar (stares incredulously and shouts).   Why, but it's——

Hilda (breaking out in jubilation).   It is the master builder himself!

Mrs. Solness (screams with terror).   Yes, it is Halvard! Oh, my great
God——! Halvard! Halvard!

Dr. Herdal.   Hush! Don't shout to him!

Mrs. Solness (half beside herself).   I must go to him! I must get him
to come down again!

Dr. Herdal (holds her).   Don't move, any of you! Not a sound!

Hilda (immovable, follows SOLNESS *with her eyes).*   He climbs and
climbs. Higher and higher! Higher and higher! Look! Just look!

Ragnar (breathless).   He must turn now. He can't possibly help it.

Hilda.   He climbs and climbs. He will soon be at the top now.

Mrs. Solness.   Oh, I shall die of terror. I cannot bear to see it.

Dr. Herdal.   Then don't look up at him.

Hilda.   There he is standing on the topmost planks. Right at the
top!

Dr. Herdal.   Nobody must move! Do you hear?

Hilda (exulting, with quiet intensity).   At last! At last! Now I see him
great and free again!

Ragnar (almost voiceless).   But this is im——

Hilda.   So I have seen him all through these ten years. How secure he stands! Frightfully thrilling all the same. Look at him! Now he is hanging the wreath round the vane.

Ragnar. I feel as if I were looking at something utterly impossible.

Hilda. Yes, it is the impossible that he is doing now! *(With the indefinable expression in her eyes.)* Can you see any one else up there with him?

Ragnar. There is no one else.

Hilda. Yes, there is one he is striving with.

Ragnar. You are mistaken.

Hilda. Then do you hear no song in the air, either?

Ragnar. It must be the wind in the tree-tops.

Hilda. I hear a song—a mighty song! *(Shouts in wild jubilation and glee.)* Look, look! Now he is waving his hat! He is waving it to us down here! Oh, wave, wave back to him. For now it is finished! *(Snatches the white shawl from the Doctor, waves it and shouts up to* SOLNESS.*)* Hurrah for Master Builder Solness!

Dr. Herdal. Stop! Stop! For God's sake——!

[*The ladies on the verandah wave their pocket-handkerchiefs, and the shouts of "Hurrah" are taken up in the street below. Then they are suddenly silenced, and the crowd bursts out into a shriek of horror. A human body, with planks and fragments of wood, is vaguely perceived crashing down behind the trees.*]

Mrs. Solness and the Ladies (at the same time). He is falling! He is falling!

[MRS. SOLNESS *totters, falls backwards, swooning, and is caught, amid cries and confusion, by the ladies. The crowd in the street breaks down the fence and storms into the garden. At the same time* DR. HERDAL, *too, rushes down thither. A short pause.*]

Hilda (stares fixedly upwards and says, as if petrified). My Master Builder.

Ragnar (supports himself, trembling, against the railing). He must be dashed to pieces—killed on the spot.

One of the Ladies (whilst MRS. SOLNESS *is carried into the house).* Run down for the doctor——

Ragnar. I can't stir a foot——

Another Lady. Then call to some one!

Ragnar (tries to call out). How is it? Is he alive?

A Voice (below in the garden). Mr. Solness is dead!

Other Voices (nearer). The head is all crushed.——He fell right into the quarry.

Hilda (turns to RAGNAR *and says quietly).*   I can't see him up there now.

Ragnar.   This is terrible. So, after all, he could not do it.

Hilda (as if in quiet spell-bound triumph).   But he mounted right to the top. And I heard harps in the air. *(Waves her shawl in the air, and shrieks with wild intensity.)* My—my Master Builder!